TRETOWER TO CLYRO

TRETOWER TO CLYRO

Essays

KARL MILLER

Quercus

First published in Great Britain in 2011 by

Quercus
21 Bloomsbury Square
London
WC1A 2NS

A CIP catalogue record for this book is available
from the British Library

ISBN 978 0 85738 580 2

Text designed by Ron Costley
Typesetting by Ellipsis Digital Limited, Glasgow

Printed and bound in Great Britain
by Clays Ltd, St Ives plc

CONTENTS

ACKNOWLEDGMENTS

I am grateful, for permission to reprint, to the editors of the journals from which chapters of this book are drawn. The sources are as follows. Chapter Two appeared in the American magazine *Raritan*, Spring 2002; Chapter Three in the *Times Literary Supplement*, 8 December 2006; Chapter Four in the journal *Changing English*, April 2007; Chapter Five in the *TLS*, 6 April 2007; Chapter Six in the *TLS*, 19 December 2008; Chapter Seven in the *TLS*, 6 February 1998; Chapter Eight in the *TLS*, 12 November 1999; Chapter Nine in the *TLS*, 20 January 2006; Chapter Ten in the journal *Studies in Hogg and his World*, No 18, 2007; Chapter Eleven in the *TLS*, 24 October 2008, Chapter Twelve in the journal *Scotlands*, 5.1, 1998; Chapter Thirteen in the *Scottish Review of Books*, Vol. 4, No 3, 2008, and in *Raritan*, Spring 2009; Chapter Fourteen in the *TLS*, 24 September 2010; Chapter Fifteen in the *TLS*, 9 October 2009; Chapter Sixteen in *Raritan*, Spring 2010.

'Landscape is my religion,' said Norman MacCaig. Landscape and, as he might have added, the natural world. I should acknowledge the importance of his verse for some parts of this book. Since my distant youth I have drunk from his poems and his places, those of the city of Edinburgh and those of his Edenic Assynt in the Western Highlands of Scotland.

KM

From left to right, Andrew O'Hagan, Karl Miller and
Seamus Heaney on the Aran Islands.

FOREWORD

THE EXCURSIONS

'You'd better take an interest in the earth and the air, for your own poor body will go there some day.' That was the sort of wisdom that used to come with free school milk in the average Scottish primary school. I remember the blizzard around the classroom the day Mrs Wallace said it to me, a snow-scene dense enough to make the end of James Joyce's 'The Dead' appear like a moment's inclemency. The poet Hugh MacDiarmid had a feeling for the freezing lives of sheep, and he resurrected, or to some extent invented, the words that would capture the rude nature of the Scottish snowstorm, calling it the 'yowdendrift', when snow is blown across the fields at speed, or the 'yow-trummle', the ewe-tremble, when the shorn animals are seen to shiver and quake as the snow falls and they catch their death.

Two decades ago, when I came down from a suburban version of those pastures to work at the *London Review of Books*, the editor Karl Miller gave voice to a certain Scottish distrust of hopefulness when it came to matters of life and death and nature and deadlines. What Clive James called 'Karl's comic engine' was often chugging away, and I, for one, believed there was a puff of the auld schoolroom in the way he made his editorial way. From the start, there had always been versions of pastoral in his sense of what connected the voices of literature to the shape of the land, and even the urban writers he likes – Kingsley Amis, for instance – were filled with a sense of hinterland, or winterland, of childhood places and beginnings, the wellsprings of a psychology, a language, or a style. Many a powerful writer, in Karl's estimation, could reveal a country source, a little Scotland or Ireland or Wales, running from a high and forgotten place into the urban reservoir of their talent. Everyone was a little like Charles Foster Kane, who could speak of 'Rosebud', a key friend from the long lost winters of memory.

MacDiarmid was crucial, and so was Seamus Heaney. The two names came together in the office one day when the paper was being put to bed. Karl is the only editor I've ever known who edited the poems as if they were prose. It wasn't beyond him to suggest the removal of lines or the scrapping of stanzas – to say nothing, on a good day, of the scrapping of an entire poem – and this day he was reading, with his nose about two inches from the page, a galley of Seamus's poem in tribute to Hugh MacDiarmid, 'An Invocation', which was due to appear in a forthcoming number. He asked me if I could see my way clear to getting Professor Heaney on the phone. (Seamus was then teaching at Harvard.) I could only hear one side of the conversation, but it pretty much went like this:

'Seamus, I'm very grateful to you for giving us the advantage of having your excellent poem in aid of my auld acquaintance Hugh MacDiarmid in the paper. We weren't the best of friends or anything but he was certainly very good as a poet and so on, don't you think? Yes. Well, listen, my dear. The problem is this. We're delighted with the poem but there's a mistake in it.'

('A mistake?' I imagined Seamus saying. 'We can't have mistakes in the *London Review of Books*.')

'Well,' said Karl, 'it seems like a mistake to me. The thing is you have this thing about MacDiarmid's "chattering genius".'

('Yes?')

'Yes. That's wrong. I'm from Scotland myself, Seamus. [They'd been friends for thirty years.] I'm from Scotland. You once said sheep *chatter*. And I can tell you Scottish sheep don't chatter – they *blether*. Surely you mean MacDiarmid's "blethering genius"?'

Amendments were duly made and the friendship continued, and continued to broaden, I would say, over the landscape that lies between Ireland and Scotland and London, where both men did their publishing work. Friendship may be a bulwark against the passing of time, but it may also be a vessel on which to journey over the years, and they took on other passengers along the way, of which I was one. I suppose it could be said, without controversy, that we each had an interest in the grounds of literature and in the ground itself. Since the years when first I got to know these men, the landscape of these islands has been transformed, and yet it has, like a respectable ghost, somehow nobly survived the transformation. A few years before we set out on these rural rides – journeys which come into this book of essays, and proffer a view of country matters – I had reported from the farms then witnessing a holocaust in their own midst. Farmers in the Lake District were killing their sheep and burying them in Wordsworth's hallowed sods for want of the fuel-money to take them to market. And the foot-and-mouth epidemic was wiping out herds bred over centuries in Wales. Small farmers, whelped on Common Market subsidies and John Constable idylls, were now being priced out of existence by conglomerate agri-business and Tesco's. This all happened to the country as Karl was homing in on these essays and testing the pulse of the rural ethos. In time, the three of us – Karl, Seamus and I – decided to go out there and see what we could see. I believe it became a journey of minds, excursions into the past of literature as well as into the present-day of friendship, and you might say we tripped on discoveries without quite knowing we were looking for anything. The literary jaunt is a habit that may have gone out of style, but we went on these trips as a way of spending time in company with people who shared our quieter interests, no more, no less. We all live in cities, yet we dived into rurality – in advance of this book, in advance of a novel of mine featuring talking animals, and in advance, by and by, of Seamus's volume of poems, *Human Chain*, a book that might show a return to his own rural backlands – and what I believe we found on these trips were new beginnings, fresh shoots, as well as a veritable cairn of endings. To my mind our journeys were filled with endings, along with the perhaps concluding notion that nature may be larger than memory. The hills of the Scottish Borders seemed to say so, as did the trees around Abergavenny and the stones of the Aran Islands.

Scotland

It was about seven in the morning when we set out. Karl Miller opened his door in Chelsea and I stepped inside the house and immediately we started talking about the drive. 'There's no need to look so fresh-faced,' he said. 'Anybody would think you were actually happy at the prospect of 500 miles at the wheel. Eh?'

'I'm not sad about it.'

'Yes. Well. Not being sad is one of your habits. Don't think I haven't noticed it before now.' It was July and he was wearing a seersucker jacket, a rather punctured jumper, blue trousers that stopped short of his sneakers, a Panama hat, and he was holding on to a cane. 'I apologise for the delinquent Edwardian look,' he said. 'I can't help it.'

We stopped at a service station near Lichfield and Karl demanded two cakes. 'Let's see which of us can make Seamus say something bad about somebody,' said Karl, with his best comic grin. 'The winner gets a prize.' We went to the loo and Karl situated himself at the farthest-away urinal. We met up at the hand-drying machine and when I looked up at him he was wearing a very rueful smile and peering over his glasses. 'It's a well-known fact that these driers don't work,' he said. 'In the history of the world, nobody has ever got dry hands from one of these hand-drying machines.'

Driving north through England, you have a great sense of real experience fighting against heritage. There are brown signs directing you off the road to crucial destinations, but, in Cumberland for instance, the land is the great, immoveable feast, and the clouds were scudding over the top. 'People get hot and bothered about Wordsworth,' said Karl, 'but didn't he turn out to be a Tory minister in favour of nuclear bombs and stomping the poor?' A while later, we saw a sign for Ecclefechan. I knew it was where Thomas Carlyle was born

and Karl thought the town might offer the chance of a sandwich. We slipped off the motorway and inched through the
ordered trees to the town, which seemed like it had been put
to sleep some time ago. Clothes were flapping on the washing
lines, but nobody was around and the only sound was of the
distant motorway. Birds were resting on the cottage roofs.
The sky was totally blue and we stopped the car beside the
town's monument to the sage of Chelsea. 'There he is,' said
Karl. 'Thomas Carlyle. High and mighty in his coat of
verdigris.'

Ecclefechan used to be a bright country town. Nowadays
it has no sandwiches and if it has hotels, they were hiding
from us. 'No wonder Carlyle lit out for Carlyle Square in
London, or whatever it was called,' said Karl, looking out. 'A
bit sad.' It had that special Scottish ennui that can take over
in the afternoon – the slow sense that life must be elsewhere
– but we got back on the motorway and headed further and
further north.

Then to Ayrshire. We got to Montgreenan House Hotel in
Kilwinning around five o'clock, to await Seamus's arrival. It
filled me with a great unexpected pleasure to be there, to see
Karl – so much of London to me – amongst the back roads
of my own childhood county. I was tired from the drive though
and went up to my room immediately, where I fell asleep and
began to dream about Thomas Hardy. I woke with Heaney
knocking at the bedroom door. He was great in a brown tweed
suit, his face lighting the hall with expected mirth. 'That's
some driving you've done,' he said. 'There's a dram in it for
you and we'll be downstairs.'

Karl always imagines, in the Edinburgh style, that a beer

means a half pint, but Seamus is a proper drinker and you see pints when he's around. We took our drinks into the garden at the front and I showed Seamus the gap in the trees and the beauty of Ailsa Craig, the rock that stands between Ireland and Scotland. 'When Keats walked this coast he felt it followed him,' I said. 'There's a wee sonnet of his, written in 1819.'

> Hearken, thou craggy ocean-pyramid!
> Give answer from thy voice, the sea-fowls' screams!
> When were thy shoulders mantled in huge streams?
> When, from the sun, was thy broad forehead hid?

Robert Burns was lit on a number of times. Karl, since he first began publishing Seamus in the *New Statesman* in the 1960s, always felt there was a clear affinity between Burns and Heaney. They were both the sons of farmers and they both took up the pen, allowing nature herself to oxygenate the mind and inflect the morals. Seamus was keeping his counsel on that, but he'd always loved Burns, too, and appreciated the way the Ayrshire poet had brought the force of country wisdom to the modern mind. Burns's 'birl and rhythm', as Seamus put it in a poem to the ploughman, 'was in my ear' from the start. It was a rhythm in which human invention is married to seasonal habits. Burns knew the mosses, waters, slaps and styles of his own country places, and we had them very much in mind as well as in view during the days of that trip to Scotland.

At Auld Alloway Kirk the rain was off for a minute and the ruined church showed a tree growing in the nave. Even in Burns's day it was ruined. The lichens were orange that month, and their profusion gave many of the graves an orange tint. 'Look,' said Karl, 'the hellish glow from the coven in "Tam o' Shanter" has seared the gravestones.' Seamus bent down at one of the stones near the gate, the one where Burns's father is buried. Karl was further back, examining the hiero-glyphs. 'Is this Adam hiding his nakedness?' asked Karl.

'No,' said Seamus. 'I think he's exposing it.'

'But didn't he eat the apple and become ashamed?' said Karl.

We were all thinking of the first garden, of Eden, the scene of the crime and the place of banishment. Maybe that's where all pastoral investigations must begin: with a tree that repre-sents the knowledge of good and evil, and with human ambition. The trees in Alloway suddenly seemed heavy with rain. Seamus was busy still with the father's grave when Karl came up behind him. They studied a quote from Addison. Part of the enjoyment was watching how stimulating the country setting was to my friends. They stood among these graves and gave life to new associations. Another day, another year, Seamus would think of the *Aeneid*, the journey in some of its books to the hallowed place. But in that Ayrshire grave-yard they thought of local poets. Karl spoke of James Hogg and Wordsworth and what the land might give to a writer who looks to the earth to speak.

At Burns's birthplace now they have something called the Tam o' Shanter Experience. It is a performance space, a café, a shop, and a place for exhibitions, the kind of venue friendly to schoolchildren and bus runs. We stood outside and Karl smiled at Seamus and sort of winked, turning his attention to Seamus's woollen suit.

Miller: 'Is that an Irish suit?'

Heaney: 'It's like that. I can't be seen without my Confirmation suit.'

Miller: 'Soon there'll be the Seamus Heaney Experience.'

Heaney: 'That's right. It'll be a few churns and a confessional box.'

I asked Seamus how the country folk around where he grew up in County Derry reacted to him being awarded the Nobel Prize. 'Ignored it for the most part, I'm sure,' he said. 'But after the Stockholm Intervention, a certain Jackie Graham of the local grocery shop in Bellaghy wanted to open a Heaney Museum – "It'll be good for you and good for us," he said.' Seamus didn't stand in his way and made sure some manuscripts and posters were put into the fellow's hands. It made me think of another Burnsian model: writers who are famous and lionised in the city are more likely to be found notorious in the country.

Curving down through the basin of the Doon Valley, we drove into the Scottish Borders. I was still thinking about city clamour versus the rural idyll. Was the genuine sound of Celtic poetry always to be found in the glen? A central voice in Karl's essays has always been James Hogg, 'the Ettrick Shepherd'. Hogg was an event in literary Edinburgh, a star of *Blackwood's Magazine* and an impersonator of literary types. But his reputation relied on his persona as a plaid-wearing sheep-wrangler at one with the pulse of country concerns. Scottish literature offers a perfect example of rustic genius in Hogg, and Karl has written about him in the past with a fierce and beautiful instinct for seeing the pressures, and the manners, that ambition might set upon the rustic imagination.

By Cappercleuch we turned and saw St Mary's Loch, a

beautiful, flat mirror beneath the brown and green of the hills. This is where you find Tibbie Shiel's Inn, thus described by the famous Christopher North (the pseudonym of John Wilson) in the *Noctes Ambrosianae*: 'A wren's nest round and theekit moss – sae is Tibbie's; a wren's nest has a wee bit canny hole in the side o't for the birdies to hap in and out . . . a cosy bield this o' Tibbie's.' Before we hap into Tibbie's – a bield that turned out to be less cosy than in former days – we might pause over the mention of the *Noctes*. This series of imaginary colloquies appeared in *Blackwood's* between the years 1822 and 1835, and they represent, in a way that might be called germane to the pleasure of the volume you are holding in your hands now, a new negotiation between city habits and rural wisdom – between the literati and the rustic folk – that was to find fair play in literature. The colloquies derive their name from Ambrose's Tavern, where our characters would appear and disappear in the dark hours, a hotel which stood at the east end of Princes Street, in a place which – as Walter Scott's biographer Lockhart remarked – had only recently stopped being 'considered as the country by the people of Edinburgh'. The negotiation with rustic elements was seen to be an eternal as well as an entertaining problem. But let it be remembered, as your three modern travellers approach the door of Tibbie Shiel's, that this was the place where such hot argument found its comfort zone, among the ancient yew and sycamore. The *Blackwood's* boys would come here to liquefy their rhetoric among the hills and by the lochs, and they often appeared, as *dramatis personae*, and in disguise, in the magazine pieces. Among these men, on their ambrosial nights, there was a perfect, ongoing performance of the pastoral metamorphoses that was known to Shakespeare and which might in itself comprise the mossy fundament of literature. (It's the greatest theme in Scottish literature, next to doubles, a previous subject of Karl Miller's.) It is not national glory that haunts Scotland, but the myth of the verdant childhood, the trauma of Eden Abandoned. The literary symbols of Scotland are thereby Robert Burns, a ploughman poet, and Peter Pan – again, the name will give the clue – a boy from an eternal garden who never grows up. The characters who gathered in *Blackwood's Magazine* found such questions to be thrilling. 'Although founded to some extent on the actual, they are in the highest degree idealised,' wrote the editor Ferrier when the *Noctes* were collected in book form. 'James Hogg in the flesh was but a faint adumbration of the inspired Shepherd.' We see the rustic man clear and prompt in the city journal, ready and able to represent a notion of universal humanity. It is a theme of Karl Miller's writing, how the city has always shown a tendency to borrow a notion of human essences from the country, and we now follow at Miller's back, in 2006, as he enters out of the 'forest charms' once described by James Hogg into the modern snuggery of Tibbie Shiel's. There were evening echoes of previous discussions, the lint of long-ago *jeux d'esprit* floating in the air by an open fire.

Another night, another trio. We entered from a smirr of rain, snoking for supper. It turns out supper was something that happened in the glen before 6.30 p.m. A lady in a white lab coat emerged to remind us of the fact. The phrase, 'You'll have hud yer tea, then?' is not unknown in Scotland's eastern quarter. I didn't hear it much as a child, being from the other coast, but I knew of it and have always thought it a strange anomaly: the bad-tempered reverse of the nation's inborn hospitality. Karl is better than Seamus at handling difficult customers, though the Professor, as much as your own correspondent, was amused to see the Bard wearing an aspect altogether more stern, not to say furious, than his customary smile and glint. With a huff and a puff, a round of fish was offered. We drank Talisker – the Skye malt, favourite of Robert Louis Stevenson – and tore the strips off some small sachets of tartare sauce whilst we heard how annoying it was to see Czech incumbents at the local church. Seamus has small tolerance for intolerance, so he drank his whisky, rolled his eyes, and went to bed. We were all soon enough in our own rooms, and I looked at the moon on the Loch. I'd borrowed from Karl a manuscript version of his essay on Burns, and the day ended for me with these words, a bleeze from the minds in the house. 'Over the sea, in Northern Ireland, Ayrshire's neighbour, Burns's verse was seized upon from the first, and no poet in English or Scots is closer to Burns than Seamus Heaney, who has written about him with exceptional insight. Each is of the soil and of the country. Heaney's early poem about his father digging directs a homage that can also be caught in the solemn music of "A Cottar's Saturday Night". With no wish to atavise the two and freeze them at the spade or plough, it might be said that the vitality of one attests to the vitality of the other, each trenching upon a pre-industrial common ground.'

Mid-morning the next day we were standing beside the grave of James Hogg at Ettrick Kirk. The rain was heavier now, and the only sound was of daws cawing on the trees, and a single blackbird came with its orange beak to sit on a gravestone two rows over and watch us. It was one of those memorial yards where everything seems watchful – the trees, the church, but even the stones themselves, whose chiselled words look for God in all of this, and which seem anxious, like all epitaphs, for eternity.

Heaney: 'I don't know what the protocol is – to visit the jacks inside the church or go outside. Outside, I think.'

Miller: 'Watch out. There's police in these parts that go in search of pee-takers and revolutionaries.'

Hogg's grave was lavishly carved and had a harp at the centre of all the words and recommendations.

Miller: 'That was his seal, that harp. It's remarkably ostentatious, isn't it?'

Heaney: 'Aye. And there's a Grieve over there, forby.'

I asked why Hugh MacDiarmid had been so keen to be a Hugh not a Christopher, and a MacDiarmid not a Grieve.

Miller: 'It was Edwin Muir's great joke about MacDiarmid's acolytes. "Men of sorrow and acquainted with Grieve".'

Lichen covered the wet stone. We went inside the church and signed the book. The place seemed recently abandoned. A bible was open on an oak table and dead flowers stood next to the baptismal font. A group of drawings were pinned to a board. Seamus looked at them. 'I thought they were meant not to have any images in these places,' he said. 'Just the landlord.' He looked at the bust of Francis Lord Napier of Ettrick before he examined the pulpit.

Heaney: 'It's high up. The first church I went to in Bellaghy was just a pulpit sticking out of a wall.'

Miller: 'It is high up. Halfway up to heaven.'

Seamus climbed up to the pulpit. 'My God,' he said. 'Why

hast thou forsaken me?' The trees seemed to have something to say at the window. The countryside was pressing again on the universal. Someone's spectacles sat on a book called *Mission Praise*. The carpet was claret-coloured and you wondered why it always needed to be so cold in the house of the Lord. From the top, Seamus quoted Thomas Hardy – 'The Darkling Thrush, 31 December 1900.' He spoke of a visit he and Marie made to Stinsford Churchyard at Hogmanay in the year 2000. 'The new millennium,' I said.

Miller: 'The poem's first title was "The Century's End".'

Heaney: 'Aye. We went to pay tribute.'

Outside the church you could still hear the talk of the jackdaws. You could wonder what gravestones and churches were for, except their presence seemed to bring something good to the glen, to this cup of land between the imposing hills.

'It's so quiet in here,' I said. And the poet's voice rose up and seemed to recuse the beams from their own dampness. Hardy's lines had found a warming Irish demeanour.

> The land's sharp features seemed to be
> > The Century's corpse outleant,
> His crypt the cloudy canopy,
> > The wind his death-lament.
> The ancient pulse of germ and birth
> > Was shrunken hard and dry,
> And every spirit upon earth
> > Seemed fervourless as I.

'That's a warm voice, Seamus,' I said.

'Well, the long day wanes, as the master said.'

We were only just beginning with burial sites. Graves and their words, stones and their epitaphs, lie everywhere in our experience of the Celtic countryside. A graveyard is a park. In the city it is often a bucolic haven between the buildings, a place of rest and flowers and pastoral shrines. During our trips, we often found ourselves gravitating towards them, these pastoral corners, these memorials, as if they could not only partner our thinking about the writing past, but make a counterpoint to the liveliness that underscores friendship. So long as you're looking at a grave, you're on the right side of vitality.

Cairnpapple Hill is the only spot in Scotland I've ever been to where you can experience the country's girth, seeing the two coasts at once. The summit of Goat Fell on the isle of Arran can be seen in the west, and the Bell Rock, smack in the Firth of Forth, is clear on the other side, down to the east. Walking up to the burial mound, Karl and I were approached by a herd of cattle. 'Good, good,' said Seamus, coming up and flicking them away. 'A square-go in Arcadia.' The prehistoric henge, with its later, Bronze Age cairn, speaks of burial rituals as old as the first links in the human chain. We all thought about the dead up here – there was a whistle yet on the wind from Alloway, piping of auld acquaintance – and watching Seamus among the ancient stones one couldn't help but think again of bogs and murders:

> imagining our slow triumph
> towards the mounds.
> Quiet as a serpent
> in its grassy boulevard,

the procession drags its tail
out of the Gap of the North
as its head already enters
the megalithic doorway.

When Seamus went digging, all those years ago, in poems written before I was born, he was bound to find something of himself and maybe of his country, too, but I considered the matter afresh as we stood in the wind on Cairnpapple Hill. He was always likely to find the Grauballe Man, the muddy end of life. We are all in the end part of the earth, writers and farmers both, handling it, tilling it, being imbued by it, and one day covered.

Ireland

We were on the ferry from Holyhead. The day was grey and damp, with mist banking over the sea. As we sat in the cafeteria, Karl kept looking out the window. He said he was trying to work out where the coast was. He looked at me and showed an expression I'm not sure he's aware of having, a broad grin that often signals a joke. 'When your ancestors came over on raping missions,' he said. 'Rowing their punts. They must've had trouble knowing where to find the bare-footed maidens.'

O'Hagan: 'Yes. The ancestors. In their punts. They would've had strict instructions to look for plumes of smoke.'

Miller: 'But it's hardly the world-centre of vivacity – Holyhead, I mean.'

O'Hagan: 'There's a small amount of smoke, though.'

Miller: 'That's right. As we were driving in I saw a young man standing against a chip shop smoking a cigarette. He didn't look as if he was getting the absolute most from life.'

Jonathan Swift wrote his poem 'Holyhead' in 1727. It has fire and resentment, and a well-turned heel:

> Lo here I sit at Holyhead
> With muddy ale and mouldy bread:
> All Christian victuals stink of fish,
> I'm where my enemies would wish . . .
>
> . . . With rage impatient makes me wait
> A passage to the land I hate.
> Else, rather on this bleaky shore
> Where loudest winds incessant roar,
> Where neither herb nor tree will thrive,
> Where nature hardly seems alive,
> I'd go in freedom to my grave,
> Than rule yon isle and be a Slave.

The boat we were on was called *Swift*, after the great man. It must be said that any jokes you might make about a place – country places or otherwise – have to seem tame next to Swift's excellent savagery.

When Karl opens his diary next morning to check something, he shows me the place where he keeps a list of his illnesses, headed 'Woes'. We went to the National Library to see an exhibition on W. B. Yeats and had the odd experience of Seamus talking between us as well as on a screen that was cocooned in a booth. On the way to the National Gallery we walked under the fading sign high on a gable-end for Finn's Hotel, where Nora Barnacle was working when Joyce first met her. There was a nice wind brewing and Seamus was struggling against it. He said: 'My father used to say to us in the morning, "Get up and get the stink blown off ye."' In the National Gallery we looked at some Jack Yeats paintings and then went to the shop, where I pointed to a line of postcards featuring Seamus. He tutted. I took one down, a portrait painted by Edward McGuire in 1974. It showed a rather sullen, tousle-haired graduate of the bog. Karl immediately plucked a postcard from the display and presented it to our faces. 'Look,' he said. 'They have one of me, too.' It was a portrait of a terrifically wizen-faced old woman wearing a purple head-scarf. Title: 'The Fisherman's Mother'.

As we planned our trip to the Aran Islands, Karl ruminated on previous journeys made there by earnest individuals keen on the rustic life. 'Yes,' he said. 'They used to go up to those shoe-less natives standing apart from their clay biggins and the visitors would say: "Hello, I went to Oxford and Cambridge you know, and I would thank you for a flagon of your finest poteen."'

We began the drive west. Trying to negotiate the roads around Dublin, Seamus says, as if unconsciously, 'Everything's changed, changed utterly.'

Heaney [to Karl]: 'Do you remember your old friend Norman MacCaig's statement about MacDiarmid? He said something he said was "excessive, but not enough".'

As the fields roll by, Karl gets to talking about our target, Yeats, and Yeats's world. He says that Conor Cruise O'Brien once heard some Irish men in a country pub saying that Yeats wrote a lot of 'queer rambling stuff'.

Heaney: 'Well, there's a lot of that. But Yeats is a resource: nationalists can go to him and so can the revisionists and of course there are those who will say he and Lady Gregory co-opted the Gaelic tradition, but they also enlarged that.'

I asked if there wasn't this basic, time-worn sense of the land itself being the first and last resource. A romantic notion, or a primitive one, of the clay being everything.

Miller: 'Yes. Well, you might say it's behind the best of everything written hereabouts, and thereabouts, if you're talking about Scotland, or in Wales.'

Heaney: 'It's a point of view.'

O'Hagan [to Seamus]: 'Did you know Patrick Kavanagh?'

Heaney: 'I only spent one afternoon with him and I felt lucky to get out alive. I remember I asked him if he liked Thomas Hardy's poems and of course he took that to be a kind of insult, as if I was asking a country poet if he liked a country poet. He said to me, "Pope is a good poet!" And that just seemed to answer all the issues. But he tried the same thing on John McGahern. John told me about it and indeed he used it in a short story of his. He was in a pub with Kavanagh and Kavanagh told him to go next door and buy him a packet of fags and John decided this was a challenge and that he wouldn't go. He was something else, Kavanagh. All well known. He was always touching people for money. He once borrowed ten shillings off another writer. "Don't say anything," he said. "I don't want my wife knowing I'm in the 10 shilling class."'

Miller: 'Yes, Kavanagh is reported to have said that he wasn't an intellectual or anything, but that it was great to have a poet like Auden, with his "well-stocked mind", with his

Freudianism and other -isms. All junk of course, he said, but it does to make a blaze.'

We passed by Offaly and Seamus asked me if I knew what a BIFFO was.

'No.'

'It means a Big Ignorant Fucker From Offaly.'

Later we drove by the asylum in Ballinasloe.

Miller: 'Is it a major Irish asylum?'

Heaney: 'It would be, yes.'

I was looking out at the landscape as we drove beyond the Irish midlands. If you come from a Protestant country, where the hedges are trimmed and evened-up to within an inch of their lives, the mad tangle of Irish hedges is striking. I imagine Scotland's hedges speak of order and repression, of a land heavily demarcated, parsed, and owned, but in Ireland a certain bucolic anarchy exists, as if the land bears its own sense of history and violence. Apart from the chocolate box wilderness of the Highlands, the countryside of Scotland wears a rather tamed look, but not Ireland, which presents itself as an entity that might again revolt against the people. The landscape appears to have a mind, a vengeful one, an Old Testament one, if you think of the potato famine.

I came back to the conversation as Karl and Seamus were discussing the notion of writers being either 'branch men' or 'head office'. This came from a story Seamus was telling about T.S. Eliot. Lloyd's Bank decided to throw a party a few years ago for Mrs Eliot and Seamus went as the representative poet. Some knight or other was giving a speech and he said that Eliot wasn't the only poet ever to work for Lloyd's. Cardiff's Vernon Watkins was also very much the poet, giving a lot of time to his writing whilst refusing to take days off and preferring to come to his desk. Then again, said the gentleman, 'Watkins was a branch man and Eliot was very much Head Office.'

We stopped for lunch at a favourite place of Seamus's called Moran's. It specialises in oysters and they gave us a table to ourselves in the snug. There was a nice bottle of Alsace and we all three had chowder. Seamus once wrote a poem after coming here, called 'Oysters':

> We had driven to that coast
> Through flowers and limestone
> And there we were, toasting friendship,
> Laying down a perfect memory
> In the cool of thatch and crockery.

In the main room of Yeats's tower at Ballylee, with the shallow stream below and the light coming at the green-framed window, I looked at Seamus and Karl and suddenly had a vision of a time when they would no longer be alive, or a time when none of us would be alive. Yeats wrote about such a feeling in his poem 'In Memory of Major Robert Gregory'.

> Now that we're almost settled in our house
> I'll name the friends that cannot sup with us . . .

> . . . Or mere companions of my youth,
> All, all are in my thoughts tonight being dead.

We looked at the woods from the top of the tower: the sheer beauty of the tall trees giving out to other greens, and this sense of peace up there was unforgettable. Coincidence deepened, and we stayed the night at a house once owned by Robert Gregory near the shore. Built in the late 18th century, the house was completely beautiful: the fire roared in the grate and there were wild flowers everywhere and midges too. The couple who run the house are nice and well-liked, despite there being a certain B&B mania in the house. 'I thought he was going to be some steely-eyed English laird, endlessly finding the guests insufficiently glamorous,' said Karl of the landlord. 'He had Norman eyes.' On the road to Dooley the next morning the 'rules in the residence' raised a belated laugh, though. 'Children are out!' said Karl. 'Dogs are out! Televisions are out! If you get up in the middle of the night – don't!' There was no arguing with the hospitality, though, or the beauty of the house and the shore down there. Seamus said he regretted not calling his book *The Spirit Level* by its first title, *The Flaggy Shore*.

On our way to catching the boat to the Aran Islands, Karl was talking about writing the countryside into being. He was interested in writers who did that, who gave the land a voice. He used the word 'finesse-ful' and Seamus looked round at me. 'That's a great new word for us,' he said.

The boat to Inisheer was busy but the water was very still. I took pictures of Seamus and Karl as we crossed, and felt quietly amazed to see how transfixed they were by the water and the distance from us to the land. As we left the boat at Inisheer I could hear people whispering Seamus's name, and he is very good with that, saying hello to people. The island was so serene and filled with literary echoes. We climbed into a pony and trap at the pier and were soon off round the island. The man driving the vehicle was the very picture of robust

outdoor health, and Seamus took pleasure, he said, in the way
the fellow 'lazily whipped' the pony every few seconds. It was
Seamus who seemed best able to speak to the man, negoti-
ating the price in Gaelic – 'driving a bard bargain,' as Karl
suggested. As we trotted along the road – passing great, drystone dykes on every side, made of limestone – the man revealed
his name was Tomas Griffin. He said many on the island were
O'Flahertys ('the ferocious O'Flahertys') or O'Briens, who had
been routed by the former many years ago. There were also
a fair number of Kenneallys. Tomas Griffin gave off a powerful
sense of knowing his world: having it by heart, every person
and their history, knowing every corner of the island and how
it might have changed over the years. Every inch of Inisheer
seemed to be accounted for, marked off with stones. I'd have
said Tomas was a drinker by the weathered look of his face,
if I hadn't been more persuaded that his face was just an
outdoor face, the complexion that nature intended. Our driver
went on with the lazy whipping and near the top of a hill, as
the sea appeared calm for miles, he looked again at Seamus.
'You're the famous poet,' he said. He told us in the 1970s the
only electricity on the island was provided by generators at
the lighthouse, so they had the only TV and over 100 people
crowded in there one time to watch the All-Ireland Final. He
looked again at Seamus with a combination of shyness and
intrigue. He clearly thought the poet was a country man who
had somehow made it into the universe of electricity and television.

At the top of such a place, you can imagine, for seconds
at a time, that urban life is only a dream. It was a steep incline
and Karl had to paddle hard with the stick. We passed many

flame-top flowers on the way up before coming to a blue gate and the path up to the 15th-century O'Brien's Castle. Maybe that was another thing the city borrowed from the country: a sense of mythology and morality dancing together on the headland. Standing up there with the castle solid and the wind whistling and the light moving over the ancient stones below, you could think of Theocritus on the island of Cos, or Virgil in Arcadia, or John Synge over by, a world of fairy tales and oral ballads.

Heaney: 'The first words ever I spoke in front of an audience were in a play at my boarding college. I was playing a butler and I said, "You called, Sir?" I got a taste for it then and it never went away.'

Miller: 'Andy here was a famous dancer. He pirouetted around Glasgow.'

O'Hagan: 'That's true. I came from one of those communities where you got six of the belt if you didn't perform your *pliés* the instant you got up in the morning.'

Miller: 'We called it the "tawse" at school.

O'Hagan: 'Or the strap.'

Heaney: 'When I was teaching, I only ever used it about 4 times. One day a young fella wouldn't yield and I gave him 4 and then 2 and 2, all in one lesson. That was terrible, really.'

Looking over those fields of stones, you might be forgiven for thinking, just for a moment, that the land was all a monument. Even in the sunshine, every road was a Via Dolorosa, every yard was a graveyard, and even the daily joy of living persons was built on a heap of chippings and bones. Weirdly, it wasn't an unhappy thought as we made our way down to the beach, where an old ship lay rusted on the rocks. Out in the wilds, death is always the black backing on the mirror that allows you to see anything at all. It is always the theme, the story, the hinterland. One of the things you could feel is that writers belonged here. 'Richard Murphy was observed by a local on the island of Inishboffin, "walking around the island working the head",' said Seamus.

We had crossed over many pastures in the previous days and now it was Marie's birthday. We wanted to give her something that would also mark the journey. Seamus took us down to Francis Street where we found an inlaid ivory box with a silver frog on top, a slick little frog like the one Ted Hughes often dreamed of. Seamus took us over to St Patrick's Cathedral and we stood before Swift's grave, reading Yeats's tribute, then Pope's. I went round the corner from there and saw a plaque on the wall to Swift's servant, put there, apparently, by Swift himself. I thought this was very cheerfully democratic and said so to Seamus as we stood in the cathedral's main aisle. 'Diligence and prudence,' said Seamus. 'Well played, that man.'

Wales

Three winters passed. Life performed its duties. None of us was younger or much the wiser. We'd been thinking about Wales for some time and we set out at the start of the summer, 2010, when the trees looked ready for inspection. Seamus agreed that we should pick him up at a hotel near Birmingham Airport. We got deeply entangled in a ludicrous series of roundabouts, which Karl imagined to represent a cycle of Midlands torture unmatched since the blindings and dousings in the plays of William Shakespeare. By the Birkenhill Parkway, Seamus was standing outside his hotel next to a fire engine, as the entire human contents of the building were evacuated in a drill. Seamus was staring into space. 'Look,' said Karl, 'the Great Bucolic Contemplates Life Among the Ring Roads.'

After what might be called preliminaries – a quick and unelaborate conversation about health, loved ones, and the power of the essay to conjure with life – the fellows moved succinctly to an exchange about the poet Henry Vaughan. The car was digging through the miles towards Wales.

Miller: 'Vaughan was bilingual as a child. His favourite river was the Usk.'

Heaney: 'The Usk. Handsome word. There's a poem about the Usk by C. H. Sisson. He was devoted to this part of the world. Donald Davie once said our times needed a Dryden to drive through the centre of the whole thing. He suggested Sisson.'

O'Hagan: 'Really?'

Heaney: 'Yes. I have to say I was resistant. He translated *The Divine Comedy*. No. I was resistant.'

I later looked up the poem Sisson wrote about the Usk.

Standing beside the Usk

You flow like truth, river, I will get in
Over me, through me perhaps, river let me be crystalline
As I shall not be, shivering upon the bank.
A swan passed. So is it, the surface, sometimes
Benign like a mirror, but not I passing, the bird.

The landscape round here is green and silvery and not short of magnificent, ewes on the hills, and the hills themselves rising to great heights from nowhere. When we arrived at our hotel, the Bell at Skenfrith, there were cars parked all the way up to the castle. It had become traditional for us to be preceded at hotels by a host of naked girls. This time, in the foyer of the hotel the girls were actually gathered in their scants, about to walk the runway in the hotel's annual fashion show. Seamus smiled from ear to ear and Karl looked uncertain as to where to place himself. 'That'll do,' said Seamus, laughing into the circus. 'Top marks.' After a moment, Karl looked up, quoting from 'Tam o' Shanter'. 'Weel done, cutty sark,' he said. As we walked up to our rooms Karl stopped in the corridor and looked at us. 'Do I suddenly seem very old and doddery to you?'

Heaney: 'Not at all. Sure, look at me.'

That evening, at the Walnut Tree Inn in Llanddewi Skirrid, a small building under a giant Monmouth hill, the birds were making a beautiful racket. The sky was pink. The boys ate Dover sole with nutty potatoes called ratte, and drank a bottle of Pinot Grigio. It was true the details seemed to be mounting, on this, the third of our trips, but I feel that not only the devil but the value of the trip was there, in the detail. Conversation has its flare-ups and its exaggerations, its moments of ballet, its crushing moments, too, but I kept coming back to the thought that conversation was a fundamental in the literature of these islands. The beat of the voice and the flutter of opinion: it lay there in the literature of these countries, bound to the steady metre of walks and excursions and friendships.

We came from Abergavenny in a taxi, shrouded in trees and hills. It was like squeezing through a hole in the dark. There was light and laughter coming from our hotel, the catwalk models and their friends now hopping in the bar.

If the countryside had a mind, you reckon its default position would be amusement when confronted with the ceaseless tide of human stuff. It must have seen it all before, the coming and going, the laughter, and the darkness coming round again. When I came down to the breakfast table in the morning, you could hear the spring lambs baa-ing not far from the open windows. Wordsworth's signature belief, we might say, was that the land was imbued with the syncopations of morality. He believed human experience was captured in the flower, mirrored in the lakes, altering like the seasons, lonely as a cloud. Moreover, he saw a model of immortality in the hills. And wasn't it inevitable that Wordsworth would care about epitaphs, about words scratched into rock and scattered about the parklands? 'Without the consciousness of a principle of Immortality in the human soul,' he writes in his *Essay on Epitaphs*, 'man could never have had awakened in him the desire to live in the remembrance of his fellows . . . The first requisite, then, in an Epitaph is, that it should speak, in a tone which shall sink into the heart, the general language of humanity as connected with the subject of Death – the source from which an Epitaph proceeds; of death and of life. To be born and to die are the two points in which all men feel themselves to be in absolute coincidence.'

The grave of Henry Vaughan can be found on a hill next to the River Usk. He lies in the graveyard of Llansantffraed Church, where there are trees on every side, the trees advancing like Birnam Wood. There are words, of course, on all the graves, but more than that there are words in the air:

They are all gone into the world of light!
   And I alone sit ling'ring here;
Their very memory is fair and bright,
   And my sad thoughts doth clear.

Vaughan's grave is under a giant yew tree. It is stained with moss and lichens, its Latin phrases shaded from light. There's no obvious path up from the road, so we climbed through the grass and found the grave looking not obscure but unvisited. There's a bench to one side, with a bank of very old grave-stones – some as old as Vaughan's, 1695 – now attached to the wall for their preservation. Karl and Seamus sat on a bench and argued about the Latin on Vaughan's grave. I was pleased to be with my friends, and the day was very fine and the sky through the trees was bursting with colour. The epitaph speaks of maximum sin and an eternity of supplication before God.

Miller: 'Well, here's Vaughan. A believer. It's hard to think of you, Seamus, without belief. I find it hard not to believe you believe.'

Heaney: 'I stopped practising a long time ago, but some of it holds. If you have it as a child it gives you a structure of consciousness – the idea there is something more.'

Miller: 'I probably wouldn't go that far, but I have to say: I always believed I would see my granny again. She was good to me.'

Heaney: 'For me, my father. I'd hope to see him again, all right.'

We stayed there for a while and Seamus spoke about Eliot and the *Four Quartets*. In all this gadding about, there had been many kinds of pastoral and an easy dalliance of time past and time present, but I sensed that, for Seamus at least, this wasn't an Eliotic rose garden. It was just a place in which to rest your bones and take a breath. And that's what happened, as the light came through the leaves.

We walked down the hill and got the car and drove further on through the countryside. This really was a world of light, but also a world of making light. As we passed over the Usk it said on the radio that the name Clyro derived from the Welsh for 'clear water'. Maybe Wordsworth was right and the countryside was our guide; maybe Burns was right and the common life was everything; maybe Milton told us the truth in 'Lycidas', that the pastoral idyll was our back-story, our song, our starting place, and our end.

> Under the opening eye-lids of the morn,
> We drove a field, and both together heard
> What time the grey-fly winds her sultry horn.

But as I lift the camera above the car and let the car and three friends disappear into the woods, where castles and old habits and conversations died hard, and where afternoon tea was served before the trip home, I want to remind you that literature is always the work of men and women. The world is there, but it is how we perform in it that makes the story. I am happy to introduce Karl Miller's essays with a private story of journeys made in search of the country spirit. I believe we found it, and that these essays lift the matter, giving a sense of what literature can do to enrich our habitations. And so the car goes off and the forest encloses the whole. Yet everything remains. The rocks and mountains of Wales were there on every side, and, further back, the places of Ireland, and further still, Scotland. We passed over roads and fields, 'slaps and styles', and found human character in the middle of nowhere and vitality in the graveyards. It is all there in a blade of grass and in our own passing.

Andrew O'Hagan

I

COUNTRY WRITERS

The word 'pastoral' has referred both to the work of writers who live in the country and to the work of writers who don't, but are moved to inhabit a country of the mind, and there are many people now for whom the generic practice, with its traditional devotion to the ideal, the exemplary, the imaginary, the fantastic, has become archaic. It would be a pity to lose the word, if only for the nostalgic cravings it commemorates, but it can be hard to apply to modern work. There are country books which do not invite it, and there are pastorals which barely mention the countryside. The 'versions of pastoral' described by William Empson in 1935, in his book of that name, were to suggest both how useful and how elusive the term could by then be.

It seems fair to say that literature's countryside has become less dream-like than it was in the heydays of the pastoral genre: the books in question tend to embody the first-hand experience of a surviving countryside. Several of the essays in this book are about recent novels which concern and proceed from country lives. They also proceed from Scotland and the Scottish diaspora of Canada and Nova Scotia, from Ireland and England and the Anglo-Welsh Borderland, and from America. Some of their authors' names begin with a 'Mac'. Not all of these particular authors are country people. To this gang of patronymics, however, can be assigned a wizardry of the rural and at times of the ancestral. I already knew, when I came to read the various writers discussed here, that the countryside, which has often been deemed incapable of literature, has continued to write it, and I was to become aware of the new ruralism, both discursive and imaginative, which has been identified in Britain.

Town and country are categories which have drawn much of their meaning from the antithesis and warring duality they are taken to represent. In the course of the 19th century, when Marx and Engels were to speak of its idiocy, rural life elsewhere occasioned a nostalgia for its imagined past and a warm embrace of pastoral modes in literature; the bourgeoisie could be credited, even by Marxists, with rescuing people from rural life, but there would be bourgeois who wished to celebrate it and go there for weekends.

Raymond Williams's book, *The Country and the City*, published in 1973, set out to historicise the English countryside, to join it to the city, as subject to the same process of capitalist and eventually imperialist control. He invokes the 'long inhumanity of city and country alike', and says enough to dissuade country-lovers from believing that there are places of refuge from the cruelty of others, and from their own. Some versions of pastoral are seen as politic and inauthentic.

He grew up in the Anglo-Welsh Borderland, and his imagination was never to leave it. The territory, together with his family background, is present though not persistent here, in a book firmly committed to argument and generality. It's a rewarding book which is not, with its exigent abstractions, easy to read, and this exigence has a certain affinity with the stubborn, cagey English spoken by the Welsh folk in his novel of 1960, *Border Country*. 'The rhythm is an unfinished truculence.' This speech, which is remote from the one conventionally expected of the persuasive and seductive English-speaking Welsh, and which was carried over into the novel's narrative voice, nevertheless proves, in its own way, wholly persuasive. Here is a manner of speaking which makes it what it is, one of the best of Britain's country books since the Second World War, a proud, bright, funny picture of Williams's tribe, an expression of faith in the silent father at the heart of what happens. The novel's strike-breaker Meredith, a resourceful speaker of this dialect of reserve and restraint, defies his mates and goes on to defy the rail authorities on his signal-box phone. He then hangs up and sits down by an empty grate. 'To look at him, nobody would suppose that he was thinking or feeling anything.' Meredith is not a main character, but he is a force. He is far from demonised as a scab.

'By the middle of the 19th century,' Williams writes in *The Country and the City*, 'the urban population of England exceeded the rural population: the first time in human history that this had ever been so, anywhere.' And the same claim has since been made for the world at large. He also claims that 'even as late as 1871 more than half the population lived in villages or in towns of less than twenty thousand people.' By the end of the century, however, rural Britain had become 'subsidiary', the place of agriculture 'marginal'. And yet the idea of a lost rural economy is, in his opinion, false. So the country, while mattering less, still matters, and if much of the world has remained rural, it would be odd if no literature were to have come of it in modern times. Such a literature exists, and is of vital importance to the English-speaking culture of the present day.[1]

For Raymond Williams, the country lacked the innocence which is often attributed to it, and the raptures of the diarist Francis Kilvert[2] may have seemed to him beside the point, his class culpable. In 1870, in the same Anglo-Welsh countryside, Kilvert opened the book of his diaries, which, a hundred years later, Williams's book does not mention, but which belongs to the assortment of texts – journals, memoirs, fiction – thought to have served as conductors of the desire for a bygone rural life. A Francis Kilvert Society was formed, as was a Gilbert White Society, with both men attracting a 'Janeite' devotion – to match the reading of Jane Austen's novels which enrols them in the same assortment of texts.

Kilvert was not expressly nostalgic, though he is the cause of nostalgia in others, and could be intrigued by past times and old places. There's a fine account of a place with 'a strange quaint old world look which took one back a hundred years. The Sleeping Beauty might still be sleeping there and waiting for the magic touch and kiss of the Prince.' A peacock preens, and rattles its feathers.[3] What generally compels him, however, is what is going on in Clyro in the 1870s – his here and now. The diaries have the contrasting aspects of a countryside which is both garden and place of work, both a paradise and a site of suffering. He strongly wished to memorialise the people, animals, plants and weathers of his parishes, and he did it very well: a tall black-bearded Anglican priest, with a passion for Wordsworth and Burns, and an interest in James Hogg,

he was a romantic *solitaire* who gave himself both to his countryside and to his priest's pastoral duties, a pastoralist twice
over. His parishes were in the old county of Radnorshire, with
its element of a wild Wales, and in Wiltshire, where the English
class system was more deeply entrenched and at times grotesque.
In 1871, the population of Clyro in Radnorshire was 842.
Raymond Williams was born in a nearby hamlet some fifty
years later. Shortly after marrying, Kilvert died young, of peri-
tonitis, in 1879.

His was an eidetic countryside – one of glimpses and effects.
It's like the countryside which you'd think must flash on the
inner eye which Wordsworth called 'the bliss of solitude'. The
diarist records: 'The deep, dark river, still and glassy, seemed
to be asleep and motionless, except where a leaf or blossom
floated slowly by.'[4] The poet and cleric William Barnes, whom
Kilvert visited, spoke of such images in terms of a second
sight: there was 'a farm house in a hollow that I had passed
by some time before. I knew nothing about the house or the
people, but it haunted me. I saw the place in a vision.'[5] You
do not have to be second-sighted, or pious, to have such
visions, and they can, of course, relate to urban settings too.
But they are, I'd imagine, among the main ways in which the
country acts on us, whether or not we live there. Kilvert chose
to live there, and loved it. He went to London (no longer a
formidable journey) for concerts and exhibitions, but didn't
want to linger, and he failed to jump at the chance when
sounded out as a possible chaplain in Cannes. His diaries teem
with landscape, with prose passages of Turner and Constable,
with beasts, birds, waters, snows, floods, tears, kisses, romps,
madness, tuberculosis, drink, fights, with the neuralgic 'face-

aches' of the period which went with his failing health. His eyes were in some unspecified way damaged – disfigured, as he felt.

He kept falling in love. He could fall in love at sight – in a flash. There was Daisy, who never married and later said: 'I thought Mr Kilvert passionately loved me, but I suppose I was mistaken.' She was succeeded by Kathleen and Ettie, somewhat concurrently. He wondered whether his damaged eyes might put a girl off. In more than one case, he may have been assessed by gentlemen fathers as a poor match, and in Daisy's case he might have been more persevering. Some of the girls were nubile, others not. 'Gipsy Lizzie', whom he taught in his school, and who seems to have been one of 'these wild rich natures, these mountain beauties', may perhaps have been Welsh. 'Ah Gipsy,' he sighs. 'May all God's angels guard you, sweet.'[6]

He took an interest in whipping. It was a word which was frequently, and often quite casually, employed by Victorians. At one point naughty little Fanny Strange was held down by her mother while her brothers flogged 'her naked bottom as hard as ever they were able to flog her'. The following day Kilvert called on the liar and thief and found her feverish but chastened, her self-will broken. 'Her parents have very wisely not spared her nor the rod.' On another occasion he was swinging a little girl who slipped off the seat and amused the spectators with an absence of drawers. 'Her flesh was plump and smooth and in excellent whipping condition.' 'Poor child,' he muses, 'I shall never see the elms on the Tor Hill now without thinking of the fall of Hebe.'[7] These two passages do not figure in the selection from the diaries done by David

Lockwood in 1992. One aspect of such disclosures, and of such omissions, is the sense they give that Kilvert was franker and more physical than many of his contemporaries are now perceived to have been, and than some of their successors. He was so far from stereotypically Victorian as to be ready to walk naked from the waves like Odysseus, under the gaze of various Nausicaas.

Nothing said in the published diaries makes him what is now known as a paedophile priest, and he was more marriageable than his contemporary, Lewis Carroll. Members of the Kilvert Society would appear to have been disturbed by his 'dark' side, while inclined to play it down, persuaded that 'there is not a trace of viciousness' in the story told of the swing mishap, a story 'which is characteristically ingenuous'. His dark side was apparent, though, to female friends, who are unlikely to have considered him ingenuous. The diaries overflow with joyfulness, almost to the point of idiosyncrasy; he was, as V.S. Pritchett has observed, 'strangely ecstatic'. But 'he had not always been a happy man', according to his niece, herself a writer, who felt that the public should be spared the whole story of Kilvert and who destroyed and sequestered sizable portions of his manuscripts. 'You will think I have done a very naughty thing, I have burnt all the diaries,' she explained to William Plomer. The diaries had already been censored by Kilvert's wife when Plomer made the three-volume selection – from 22 notebooks – which came out in 1938, 1939 and 1940: a further censorship was now inflicted by the niece. An eminent clergyman, worried about Kilvert's 'almost inordinate affection', asked another woman whether she felt 'he was a really good man.' The woman replied, after a pause:

'Yes, he was a good man; if he had not been a good man he would have been a very dangerous man.'[8]

Those worried about his displays of inordinate affection have mulled over the entry which reads: 'An angel satyr walks these hills.'[9] He is at least as mixed or uncertain as most people are, and is not wanting in complexity when measured against the run of eminent clerics, or of city-dwellers. His politics were humanly indeterminate. He looked forward to a unified Christendom, and was tolerant of Catholicism, though less so of Dissent and of a floridly ceremonial High Church. He can display a light Anglican revolutionariness. When Sarah Hicks, 'indignant tears welling in her beautiful large dark eyes', earnestly exclaims, 'Oh, it's a comfort to know that there's a time coming when no one will be able to reign over us and when we shall be as good as those who are so proud and high over us now,' he responds: 'Patience, dear Sarah, patience a little while longer. And then—' Meanwhile he disliked strikers, on occasion, almost as much as he disliked tourists, and is to be found nestling among gentlefolk, with their croquet and their bows and arrows and their inaccessible daughters.

A child, catechised as to who made the world, answered: 'Mr Ashe.' Ashe was an ordained local landowner, a connection of Kilvert's, who paints him as meanly despotic. A further catechism is described, in 1875. 'The Good Shepherd,' a child was prompted, 'leading his sheep to—' 'To the slaughter,' came the child's apt reply. A week later Kilvert watches 'the white pig lying in the moonlight at the door of his house, with the moon shining on his white face and round cheek'. Two days later he records a dream of the slaughter of a whale in Weymouth Bay, which was crimson with blood.[10] Elsewhere he is eloquently against the slaughter of birds for sport.

He got on well with the parish poor, while seeing them as such. He might not have shared the opinion of Virginia Woolf that poverty makes it hard for people to be loving or intelligent – the chances are against them. But he was squeamish about 'uneven', inter-class matings. Having carried on for years with her clergyman father's groom, a certain woman then became his wife. 'The groom's sister made the young lady's dresses and the groom used to drive the young lady to see her dressmaker. A sad story.'[11] Reader, she married him. It seems probable that Kilvert envisaged a reader for his diaries; at one stage he also attempted to publish his poems.

He was something of an adoptive Bloomsbury author, and his gentle birth and musing leafy life may have contributed to that. In a prose poem of his, Virginia Woolf is thought to have discovered grounds for revising the Bloomsbury view of the Victorians as inert and repressive, with a touch, so to speak, of the dead weight of his cousin Maria's coffin as it was laboured into Worcester Cathedral. A resemblance to a novel popular in latterday Bloomsbury circles, Alain-Fournier's *Le Grand Meaulnes*, with its mysterious rural rites, has been mooted with reference to this prose poem, in which he visits Mouse Castle and happens on four girls and a boy cavorting, as if for ever, accompanied by their father. 'They were full of fun and larks as wild as hawks, and presently began a great romp on the grass which ended in their tumbling head over heels and throwing water over each other and pouring some cautiously on their father's head. Then they scattered primroses over him.' Who could they be? They were like the spirits of the place. 'I shall always connect them with Mouse Castle. And if I should ever visit the place again I shall certainly expect to find them there in full romp.'[12] The episode is in no way exploited or exaggerated, and it imparts a sense of exclusion or loss. His is a sad story, shot through though it is with delights and with romps of his own. The reader could well feel that, whatever 'the Victorians' were like, Kilvert was thwarted, denied.

His stationary river, his snoozing pig – these sights made the diaries famous when they broke cover at the end of the Thirties. Their first fame was to coincide with the arrival of another evocation of country life, another solace for a time of war, Herbert Read's slim volume *The Innocent Eye*. Each furnished a nostalgic consolation, as did the painting of the time, with its attachment to Samuel Palmer. But Kilvert is in Clyro as he writes; he is not looking back. There is no paradise lost, no lost innocence, while Herbert Read's innocent eye is that of his youthful self, enclosed in the citadel of his family's Yorkshire farm. When his father dies the idyll is over, except as a comfort to him – no longer a countryman – in adult life. Much is made of the boy's cocooning innocence. Rereading the memoir in 2007, I was struck by this, having recently, in Radnorshire, witnessed the slow birth of a calf in the presence of a group of comprehending city children. Have children grown up since the Twenties?

Of the country books published in Britain since the Great War, Flora Thompson's *Lark Rise to Candleford* has proved a favourite. This trilogy began to appear with the outbreak of the Second World War. Her witty and beguiling book is picture-intensive, to the point of seeming synchronic at times, a gallery, a still water. One of the heroine's country sights – a view of ploughland and hedgerow – remains in her head lifelong, and is in that sense permanent, while others can be switched on when she needs them. George Sturt's *The Wheelwright's Shop* of 1923, beloved of F.R. Leavis, with its pictures of a racial-patriarchal Old England, its solemn word that what was once prized there is no longer prized, can be said to ride on the well-tempered spokes and felloes of its carts. Sturt writes of certain 'countrymen of a shy type good to meet', and Thompson remarks that the majority of people are always kind. Both of them are praisers of the past, as this might suggest, but they aren't taken in by it (which is not to deny that Thompson's enchantments can induce her to be tactful or terse, to gloss over, for instance, the evictions and disturbances caused by the enclosures that had occurred in her native village). Has the life Thompson describes been crowded out by now, made obsolete? Its quaintnesses will not upset old souls of the present day who can remember a time when books were wrapped in brown paper to protect them from their readers, and few young souls can think themselves in a lost world here, of rites and runes and lapsed customs. People are, or aren't, still skilful, and kind. Many of them still lead country lives.[13]

Twenty years after Flora Thompson's first volume, Ronald Blythe's *Akenfield* was published. Franker and more didactic, this portrait of a shy, reclusive Suffolk village owes something to the documentary art practised by 'Mass Observers' and their like in the Thirties. The time-honoured exploitation of farm labourers and their families is laid bare; a rural dean says that for several generations labourers had been 'literally worked to death'. And the nation's cruelty to animals is shown to have grown more acute under factory farming. The thought is that life in such places has got both better and worse – distinctly worse, maybe. Blythe believes that 'it is man's rightful place to live in Nature and to be a part of it,' and that 'city life fragments a man.' A woman magistrate and her benchfellows are on occasion aware, she says, that they're 'doing the wrong thing – because there is no right thing to do'. The magistrate's testament, that of the district nurse who says that 'all life was hidden' in the old days, and the account of Lana Webb – the incontinent and exuberant orphan, with her older man and her fifteen pairs of knickers a day – and of her no less endearing Gran, are among the many right things in the book.[14]

Another Suffolk village to figure in the critique of country life that came about in the last century is George Ewart Evans's Blaxhall. His *Ask the Fellows who Cut the Hay* was published in 1956, and a further edition, beautifully illustrated by David Gentleman, has recently appeared – which already suggests a remarkable longevity for a work by a student of longevity, of the traditions of the countryside and of their transformation by the technology of the 20th century. The countryside is seen as submitting to a change for better and for worse – with an enhanced emphasis, akin to *Akenfield*'s, on the second. Those were the days. As we were to continue to think, and to deny, in the decades that lay ahead. With this book, Evans is reckoned to have found his voice as a writer, a voice that made valuable use of the speech of his neighbours. Its folk wisdom is time and again worth listening to. Sleep on your right side, advises Suffolk, for the good of your heart's blood. There must be plenty of people now who would rather have this than any prescribed course of scientifically-tested anti-depressants.

These two post-war books are alike in so little resembling the well-known country books of before and after the Great War, with the exception of *The Wheelwright's Shop*, admired by Leavis, who also admired *Mr Weston's Good Wine* by T.F. Powys, which came out in 1927. It describes a sinister merry England. Et in Arcadia lust and death, and scandal. Village idiots go on about the absence, or not, of God, and light-heartedly discuss local rapes staged and rumoured by a procuress out of Jacobean drama who wishes a young neighbour 'ravished and dead'. A supernatural agency helps to enact what may sometimes be meant as an allegory of love. Powys writes that 'every man who has imagination, and who lives in the country, is sure to find out some day or other that he is a lover.'

The country books of the time have plenty of lovers. D.H. Lawrence's earlier fiction is of its period in conveying that lovers live in the country, while Mary Webb's *Precious Bane* of 1924, a considerable work in its whirling way, does the same, and is palpably of the same time. It was sent up in smiling Stella Gibbons's *Cold Comfort Farm* of 1932, in which a romantic orphan confronts a rotting, Draculan farmhouse. This upper-class gel turns her rural slum into a garden party: she has no time for 'passion' and believes that 'Nature is all very well in her place.' *Mr Weston*, with its admittedly uncertain 'Gothic' and satirical elements, may well have had a hand, it's possible to feel, in *Cold Comfort*: there, too, peasants are put in their place by a higher authority. There are books of this time which unite passion and farce, an approbation of the countryside and a derision of it. Powys's novel is both for and against it. His rustics are unseemly enough to incriminate the countryside itself, for all its scenic properties. What moves them is gossip, which has long been seen as a bucolic affliction.[15]

Precious Bane plunges back into an ultra-superstitious Old England circa Waterloo. The Cinderella who narrates gains her prince – Kester Woodseaves: 'The Maister be come!' Such a name, and the novel's florid recourse to masters, mummers, mommets, a wizard, a frowning, fascinating serial killer, might seem to make it hardly less of a burlesque than its assailant, *Cold Comfort Farm*. But then the long-duration Gothic novel has been able to smile at itself while delivering some of its strongest effects, which is more than can be said of all of its formidable males. Jane Austen's *Northanger Abbey* is both a mockery and an instance of the Gothic novel, and the same words could be applied both to *Precious Bane* and to the Stella Gibbons. Webb's purple passions and bravura descriptions are finally no joke, though, either intentional or unintentional. She means and can communicate what she is apt to overdo. Stanley Baldwin embraced the novel in 10 Downing Street, and ensured its fame. It seems that there were passions which appealed to eminence, though it took time for it to tolerate, authorise and esteem those of Lawrence. He, too, was once an English joke.

Mary Webb's earlier novel *Gone to Earth* is a piece of Georgian-Gothic gypsying, in which the dark house awaits its orphan, not for the last time, and a zeal for country life wears, not for the first time, the face of a fox. This fox is fostered by the orphan, a generally backward child of nature stranded in a landscape presented as teeming with sex. All is of the earth earthy. John Buchan, another grandee of the age, leapt to its praise, noting that it was published in the dark days of 1917. It is another of the group of fictions which surround and respond to the Great War, where country life and landscape are cherished, and a burlesque of the bucolic and the Gothic can be recognised as the thing itself, with laughter and absurdity attending a real pledge of the spirit. Some of these fictions are by stern and playful Buchan, a master of landscape, as amongst the diablerie of *Witch Wood* (1927). In Buchan too, though not in *Witch Wood*, there's an element of the self-consciously ludic.

Four years after *Gone to Earth* Lawrence produced a fox book of his own, in the shape of the final version of his long story 'The Fox'. In each of these tales the animal dies a violent death which mingles with passionate human fatalities, and a male dominance is ambivalently if often ardently displayed. In Lawrence's tale of a young man come between two women struggling with a small farm – one of them associates him with a spellbinding, masterful dog fox – it's as if men and women are sheerly different, as if no female could be a predatory wooer, a tamer of shrews. This man kills the other girl, his rival, who hasn't liked to listen to talk about 'nature', and he then embarks on a fraught marriage with her friend. Nature has murdered the friend, it would appear. Lawrence's story understands and appreciates this, and so does his encomiastic critic, Leavis. A notable forbearance is shown here by these two writers.

The later country writers of the 20th century who are discussed in the present book are not strangely ecstatic, and they do not court, though they might at times excite, a nostalgic response. All of them have lived in the country, in the green, Andrew Marvell's favourite colour.

No white nor red was ever seen
So am'rous as this lovely green.

All of them take the country seriously, but of none of them would you want to say, as you might of Kilvert, and of Marvell, that he or she was able to find a paradise in rural places, an earnest of the next life, the eternal one. Kilvert could feel chained to 'my sin',[16] while awaiting translation from this world to another and hoping for mercy. He does seem to come close to intimations of immortality, in Clyro and on his walks.

I go around with images of the country in my head, some of which resemble Kilvert's or Flora Thompson's in their benignity. Some are memories of an old acquaintance with woods and fields. Some of them appear to derive from dreams. Others again appear to be ancestral or genetic. I grew up near a farm on the outskirts of Edinburgh; further out to the south, towards the Borders, my great-grandfather had ploughed the Midlothian soil. I grew up, therefore, to be both town and country – like lots of other people, an amphibian. One of my images is of myself at 16, Youth Hostelling in the Scottish Borders. My punishing wartime Utility bike has taken me to Broadmeadows, James Hogg's native ground, where he became the Ettrick Shepherd, famous for his books and for being from the country. The sun is setting in a blue sky, amid a bank of smouldering silver clouds, and I am cuddling a newborn lamb. My relations with that lamb were and were to remain moving to me: but this was a time when nostalgia was as disgraceful as it was important, and I would just as soon have left them unspoken in any seminar of Leavis's at Cambridge on the poetry of Blake.

Seamus Heaney goes around with country pictures in his head, as readers of his poetry don't need to be told. Such pictures matter very much to his poems, for all that there's so much else there too – beyond, but not apart from, the blessed viewing and noticing that goes on. In the summer of 2007 I shared landscapes with him when we went, with Andrew O'Hagan, to County Clare, and the offshore Aran Islands, in the West of Ireland. The islands have been the countryside's Ultima Thule for several generations, and have retained their solitude, their Mycenaean drystone dykes, and their Gaelic language, which still comes into its own during the winter months. 'After the drive', Seamus wrote out for his friends a poem which might have been thought to have been written, *ambulando*, in the course of it, as an embodiment of its sights.

> And some time make the time to drive out west
> Into County Clare, along the Flaggy Shore,
> In September or October, when the wind
> And the light are working off each other
> So that the ocean on one side is wild
> With foam and glitter, and inland among stones
> The surface of a slate-grey lake is lit
> By the earthed lightning of a flock of swans,
> Their feathers roughed and ruffling, white on white,
> Their fully grown headstrong-looking heads

Tucked or cresting or busy underwater.
Useless to park and think you'll capture it
More thoroughly. You are neither here nor there,
A hurry through which known and strange things pass
As big soft buffetings come at the car sideways
And catch the heart off guard and blow it open.

The poem was, in fact, written at a previous time.[17] You might say that it predicted our trip and made it happen. I am in awe of the eye that is here, but can claim that some of its sights – the flags or long-leaved plants, the wild swans, not far from Coole and the Yeats habitat with its tower and winding stair – are mine too. They enable me to think of the poem as a homage to such sights, and a tribute to the significance that images of the country can assume.

I have dreams in which I am medieval and in a tower which tends to resemble Yeats's. I am looking out, then down, from the battlements, at the swords and bows and arrows of an approaching band of soldiers. I expect to be overwhelmed. I peer at alleys of admittance to the tower where attackers could be trapped and stabbed. I wouldn't try to persuade anyone that ancestral plights are responsible for the beleaguered dreams that appear to me, or for my many visits to ruined castles. But I do reflect that the Scottish Borders were once every bit as bloody as any region of the archipelago.

The city young with whom I stayed on the Welsh border, a little earlier in 2007, and watched the calf's birth, would some of them long to go shopping in Abergavenny, rather than scale the Black Mountains or stare at grown-ups' beautiful views: but I think they were pleased with their farmhouse, set between an Early Modern mansion – Tretower Court, once that of the Vaughan family, among them the English poet (and native Welsh-speaker) Henry Vaughan – and a Medieval tower, that of a Marcher lord, the last light of the day reaching down towards it from the direction of Clyro. I don't think they felt they were in the alien world discovered by East End evacuees during the war. The oldest and most London of these loved ones was accosted, or territorially claimed, by a collie, but he rose above nature's affront. His head was filled with music and philosophy and with pictures of his city.

I paid a visit to Clyro at this time and found it a hill-farmer's handsome village, at the foot of a high hill, part of it a tourist's mausoleum, a shrine to how things used to be and the man who wrote them down. The house where Kilvert lodged as a curate has its plaque and medallion, and its view from his window of a row of 17th-century cottages, still standing, and of the Baskerville Arms (Kilvert, with Baskervilles in their brougham among his acquaintance, knew it as the Swan) where he witnessed romps and scraps. His church stands a little above the cottages, with its ancient circular graveyard, its yews, and its photographs, inside, of a commemoration in which a replica curate smiles through his bushy beard. The trouble with tourism was perceived in the diaries, and it can compound the defects of an improved and imagined past. The trouble with nostalgia is evident in the edition of the diaries which leaves out what is reckoned to be painful.

One summer evening in 2007, at a point between its disastrous floods and an outbreak of foot-and-mouth disease, I went to see the calf whose birth had been studied by the young, and whose mother had died thereafter at the great age of 16. There the calf lay on her wisps of straw: made small by the tall bare barn, her cream coat patched with apricot, huddled or puddled on the floor, then struggling up to circle on her stilts round a melancholy pregnant cow, whom the calf went on to try to suckle, without much encouragement, and whose large face turned towards this visitor. The scene, of creatures holding on in the straw, recalled the manger of two thousand years ago, no crib for a bed. An urban scene also flashed on me. I once saw from a car, at midnight, a bag lady dragging her belongings through a Bloomsbury downpour. She looked as if she had nowhere to go but was determined to get there. She belonged to the 'nocturnal animals' – one of the unflattering names devised for the poor by Virginia Woolf,[18] who lived nearby, and was in time forced to feel unable to hold on. Animals and people, town and country, I told myself, are in this thing together. The thing is 'nature', the natural world, from which human beings have so often seen ways of removing themselves, as a special case, due to live for ever.

Just after the war, while awaiting National Service conscription in the Army, I wrote a manger story, 'The Nether Fields',[19] in which a wounded British soldier tells how he has crawled to a barn on the Alsatian border with France. He sets himself to get through, in his broken French, to a farm boy, and to have him bring help. There's a concern with communication, and with its failure, even in friendship. He watches the soldiers of his unit moving, out of touch, along a road at the far side of the fields before him – 'seeing my saviours walk singly away from me towards my death'; and 'I died' are the story's last words. This is an image of the country kind I've been talking about, and it belongs to the second of the wartimes I've been talking about, to the Second World War and its aftermath, when interest in the countryside was once more sharp. The countryside is consolatory here, though equivocally so: it's a place to be yourself, and by yourself, a place where odd fellows lie down and die, and soliloquise.

This display of rural pictures is not meant to glorify the country, or to credit its people with eidetic powers elsewhere blinded by city lights. I know that it's not exempt from the faults of its society. What it can give is hardly to be understood by unreservedly preferring it to the contemporary culture of celebrity and political dishonesty, with its wars and its worthless television programmes, a culture which has to be seen as nationwide. My belief is that what the country can give, and what 'provincial' life can give, may be caught in the fictions I'll be writing about, among many others of the present time, including the now unfolding Cumbrian comedies of John Murray, published, some of them, hard by Hadrian's Wall. Between the Great Wars, a long way to the north-east, lay the orphaned rural poverty that went into the novels of Jessie Kesson, rich in sentiment and intelligence, dominated by the 'smeddum' of young Janie. This is Scots for spirit or fire, and a man is said, elsewhere in the series of novels, to lack it: to have grown 'too old within' ever to outgrow his fear of the landlord.

A further case in point. Kazuo Ishiguro could hardly be called a country writer in the usual sense, and yet the English countryside is important to the fiction he writes. *Never Let Me Go* (2005) is a pastoral romance, a parable and a puzzle. Two boarding-school girls conduct a close friendship which

is overtaken by a cryptic process of conspiratorial organ dona-
tion (the girls are infertile, but pastoral concerns such as
'harvesting' and 'provision' may be implicit here). A new terror
is added to death, and to progressive education. One of the
girls opens the book by passing through a landscape in later
life, and studying the distant prospect of a great house stood
in a misty green. Can this be the school she'd once attended,
and which is then to occupy, in retrospect, half the book – a
'creative' boarding-school closer to the one-time arty Bedales
than to Eton? This is a countryside – full of sights and of
walks and talks – which few people can fail to have known.
The novel is as rural in its way as it is surreal, as moving as
it is ingenious.

The country and the wild are two different places, but the
country opens onto the wilderness in Britain as elsewhere, and
British wilderness books have been gathering pace in an age
of adventure and of ecological curiosity and anxiety, with Robert
Macfarlane, another Mac, a leading practitioner. Their authors
appeal to me by, as I hear, collecting pebbles, relics of an
earlier than ancient world. Country people don't always like
the wilderness, engaged as they often are in escaping it. But
it seems clear that there's a touch of it, and of the atavistic,
in certain forms of zeal for country life. Those who have green
thoughts and images in their heads may suppose that these
must in part be memories of an individual past, but that some
may be as old as any pebble, while others are as open to historical interpretation as my beleaguered tower.

Having long been subject to an uncertain polarity, town
and country have now, in some contexts at least, moved closer
together. The difference and the distance between them have

been squeezed. Business can be conducted, and journals edited
and emailed, in remote places. This will not mean that town
and country will lose their power of antithesis or their respective virtues. From a literary point of view, if literature survives,
the country may gain. But then it has been a source of inspiration and invention since spades were spades. Think of the
Lake District of 1800, where the idea of the country was transformed, and of Henry Vaughan by the banks of the Usk on
the Welsh border, and of George Herbert of Bemerton in
Wiltshire. Not long after the death of citizen Shakespeare,
these two confederate Christians wrote poems of supreme
beauty. Shakespeare, to be more precise, was recognisably
amphibious; town and country can look the same in the plays
he wrote in town, with their pictures of Warwickshire.

The landscape that runs from Tretower to Clyro, near Hay-
on-Wye, and north-west by the Usk to Brecon, was enchanted
ground for Vaughan, as for Kilvert. Son to a dubious father,
twin to Thomas, a Hermetic philosopher, Henry Vaughan,
with his Welsh tongue or second language and his Norman
forebears, was a Royalist and a gentleman, and in time a
doctor, whose house at Newton on the way to Brecon held a
litigious problem family. The sparse biographical record allows
you to imagine him tending a wealthy patient down at
Crickhowell, then summoned by Brecon magistrates over the
mispayment of maintenance amounts claimed by a hostile
daughter. The children of a first marriage were at odds with
those of a second. To a hostile son Vaughan made over the
house in which he'd spent most of his days, and then retired
to a nearby cottage. The English Civil War was over by now,
and the throne restored. Here at home was another civil war.

The King Lear of Usk had by then given up writing his devout and rapturous poems, in which he longs for an afterworld of light, while inhabiting a world lit by God's goodness; stars and stones and sunsets abide by their maker's will more steadfastly than Vaughan does, it seems. A picture from the Biblical Apocrypha would appear to have stayed with him: 'And the stars shined in their watches, and were glad; when God called them, they said, Here we be; they shined with gladness unto him that made them.' It's possible to resist his elective theology, his story of the saved soul and the lost soul: but those who like poetry must find it hard to deny the intimacy and immediacy of his raptures, with their sense of a universal fellowship. For him, night was a time for human fusses to be done with and for the divine to send messengers. His celebrated poem 'The Night' has the stanza:

> God's silent, searching flight:
> When my Lord's head is filled with dew, and all
> His locks are wet with the clear drops of night;
> His still, soft call;
> His knocking time; the soul's dumb watch,
> When Spirits their fair kinred catch.

In 2010 I went with Seamus Heaney and Andrew O'Hagan to visit Vaughan's grave, where this passage of verse was spoken. Frank Kermode had spoken it in 1986, in the course of a sermon delivered in the Chapel of King's College, Cambridge: the sermon looked into this wonderful, difficult poem, and argued that the Nicodemus of St John's Gospel is unfit for a Heaven-sent spiritual rebirth, while in Vaughan's poem the darkness of Nicodemus is changed – such are 'the uses of error' – to something antithetical, to the light-giving dark night of those whom God loves.[20]

The difference between town and country has rested in part on the assumption that country people are more exposed than others to the natural world of plants, trees, fur and feather, wind and tide, the elements. If the word 'nature' has appeared to signify a separation from the human, country people have had reason to be sceptical – or unaware – of such a separation, and to think that their affairs are bound up with other forms of life. I don't mean that those who live in cities can't think this – or that they need to be advised, as country people don't, to show a loving interest in animals and birds. I mean that the country can teach it. The sunsets over Clyro teach it. The country is often despised, as sunsets are. Despised and revered. It has given rise to definitions of humanity which should be respected, and are more likely to be respected now that we have taken to fearing our involvement in, and responsibility for, a global catastrophe, a revenge of the tides.

Town and country are both together and apart, separate and encroaching, as are man and beast. And the same can be said of England and my native Scotland. The first half of this book is about country writers, some of whom have lived in towns; much of the second is about Scottish writers, some of whom live or have lived in England, and in Canada. Scotland is both town and country, for all its rural reputation, and is subject to the convergences of the two which have always occurred everywhere in the world and are more than likely within the boundaries of a small island. *Rus in urbe*, and its converse, are ancient features on both sides of the Scottish border.

Vulpes in urbe is a current concern in London. Foxes, as ever, have been coming to town. A scene pictured for the 18th century by the poet Thomas Gray,[21] who played with their having 'stunk and litter'd in St Paul's', has been realised in modern times: one of them has been found curled up in a House of Lords locker. Hard heads seem to be in favour of a cull, on the poorly documented grounds that they have been known to attack babies. Dogs have a superior kill rate in that respect, and so have human beings. The novelist Blake Morrison likes foxes both for being other and for being us. In his millennial novel of 2007, *South of the River*, Anthea reckons she has 'inherited their violence and cunning', and smells accordingly, and appealingly.[22] Here, as in David Garnett's vulpine novel of 1922, with its full-blown vixen metamorphosis, there's the spoor of the very foxy lady.

I once embraced a lamb in the Scottish Borders, as I've already claimed. Later on, in the Sixties, sitting in an armchair in a Border farmhouse, I held in my arms a friendly young half-domesticated fox, his ears like two silk purses. Among the more remote events of my life which I can still remember in old age, these two encounters are salient: readers of my age may remember D.H. Lawrence's dictum that you live by what you thrill to – well, I have lived by these two little beasts, and I also live by the death, long ago, of my cat. I daresay these claims may seem affected or deluded, a sentimental effusion, a joke. It may be possible to tolerate them by bearing in mind what animals and their strange, unsmiling stares have meant to human beings, whose eyes can also be uncanny, how much their dogs meant to Walter Scott and James Hogg, how much the theatre of sentient life has meant to the naturalist David Attenborough; and by bearing in mind the vast cruelty inflicted on birds and beasts by human beings who fear and dislike them and by many who like them too. No wonder they are so quick to fly away from us.

Having sat with the fox, I went outside to a hedgerow where I watched a line of scarved and ponied hippies, raggle-taggle gypsies, setting off up a lane, quitting the middle class for the Appleby horse fair in the North of England; an animal lover but not a flower person, I returned to the farm, past a gnawed-at haunch in an outhouse, some dog's dinner, perhaps, or my fox's.

For most of my life I desisted from David Garnett's *Lady into Fox* because of an early squeamish dread of the anthropomorphic, of the presentation of animals as people and the other way round. Late in the day I came to it and took to it. It's a powerfully dramatised novel, and a moving one – quite against the odds as I had conceived them. A landed gentleman, used to the deference of his wife and several servants, discovers that his wife has turned into a fox. He treats her like a lady, puts her in a dress, kisses her muzzle, dines with her on chicken, and is affronted when she bloodily devours a live rabbit he has placed in her path. She had initially been 'still his wife, buried as it were in the carcase of a beast but with a woman's soul'. Soon, though, she heads for the wild and litters in an earth. He takes to visiting her and her offspring. He is at one with them. But then the local Hunt comes calling.

The novel belongs to the era when the difference between human beings and the other animals had acquired a post-

Darwinian interest and awkwardness: the era which brought H.G. Wells's *Island of Dr Moreau*, in which a mad scientist operates surgically on beasts in order to rid them of their beastliness. The hero of Garnett's novel starts out, satirically seen, as a respecter of the 'decencies', a scorner of 'mere' animals, who shoots his dogs out of hand when they threaten to get in the way of his transactions with Silvia the vixen. Then he joins the wild world by proxy: satire ceases, and the age of D.H. Lawrence may be thought to have arrived, in which more people than before have been ready to see themselves as animals, as the snake befriended by Lawrence – as birds of a feather, if you like.

'Bunny' Garnett's fox book came hard on the heels of his friend Lawrence's 'The Fox': it was published a few months afterwards, and five years after *Gone to Earth*. Ever since Aesop, foxes have been literary creatures, subject to human impersonation and inhabitation; it has often been difficult, even for beastists, to think of them as stupid. Robert Burns has a poem about a tethered fox, forced to listen in his kennel to the conversations of liberal Whig lairds, friends of Charles James Fox, on the emotive subject of freedom. The British poetry of the 20th century is full of the country and of foxes, and of shape-shiftings; and of no poet is this more true than it is of Ted Hughes, who once inscribed in a copy of his collection *Moortown* a ballad which confers a double life on a country poet who turns into a bird:

> When I was a farmer
> And walked o'er my land
> I found a gold sovereign
> Where'er I did stand.

> But now I'm a scribbler
> And nude as a carrot
> Stuck all with feathers
> And words, like a parrot.

In his poem 'The Thought Fox' Hughes is at his desk, knowing that out there in the dark treads a fox, 'coming about its own business'. Elsewhere in his poetry there's a den of young foxes, where they lie thrilled with their stench. Hughes himself is hardly less thrilled with it. Shortly after his death a grizzled old dog fox was spied in the gardens of Ladbroke Grove and deemed to be him, come back in that likeness. Poet into fox. The last of his metamorphoses.

A loving friendship with a fox was achieved in 1985 by Diana Melly, who was living at the time in a Breconshire tower not far from the Vaughans' Tretower and from Kilvert's Clyro. She called him James after the writer James Fox, and received him from a miner's wife, who'd come across two cubs, three or four inches long, whose mother was dead. James was a beautiful and intelligent ankle-nipping sprite, with sprouting ears, black paws and matching eyeliner eyes. He treated Diana as a mother, and was more at home with women than with men; there was a lesser rapport with her husband George, singer and surrealist and fisherman. Men made him nervous, but he travelled successfully to London in the pouch of a jersey. Lady and fox lived together from April to July, when it was thought best to restore James to the wild. He was placed in a reservation, from which he escaped, digging himself out from under the wire. He then disappeared, taking with him Diana's Cinderella slipper. James went missing, and is still missed. Never having met him, I miss him myself: a piece of vicarious mourning which many would regard as a bad case of the sentimental. My own view is that sentiment – 'feeling', as it was known to the 18th century, as an aspect of fellow-ship – has since then been understandably but excessively distrusted. It's true that it causes delusion and derision, and hasn't always been benevolent. Feelers can be as predatory as foxes. Fox-hunting man has feelings.

There they go, London's foxes, down my street of an evening – a mere streak, grey on grey, a trick of the half-light. But they can also be found standing in the night on front doorsteps, bold as brass, looking about them; and they can be like Robert Lowell's skunks, searching 'in the moonlight for a bite to eat'. Just the other day, Reynard was watched, on television, by a football crowd as he crossed their pitch, cutting inside like a winger, while not a winger. I love the thought of these foxes holding on in the city. Such courage. Here is a secret life which belongs to a general vigilance, that of the hidden and hunted, of killers and killed, animals and humans. These foxes are country. But then they are London too. We live in a world where it is possible for some people to think of them as displaced persons, who have their skills and should stay.

Edna O'Brien, a country writer at her delightful inception, and one who has remained in practice, has mixed feelings about the seven foxes who keep house in her Central London back-garden. They're very near, these foxes, but are far from being pets or pals. The one-time country girl feels at one with the alpha vixen, while fearing she'll be 'the death of me'.

It has long been known that people are animals. But the message continues to be ignored or denied by the majority of human beings. Philosophers were at one time eminent in denial: to think was human, and beasts were barred from that, and from the possession of souls. These days have not gone, as I say, but the message is now better-known and is the business of various schools of thought. It is reflected in the eco-feminism which speaks of a colonial mastery of nature comparable to oppressions which operate in the fields of race and gender. Here is a human master who has the power of reason, but is nevertheless dependent on a planet shared with other creatures and other forms of life.

This doctrine of mutuality and of multiple oppressions is likely to appeal to those who believe in the existence of fellow-creatures and in the prevention of cruelty to animals. Such believers may also believe what certain scientists have recently been denying: that animals – patient, prudent, violent, all too human – have minds.

These essays of mine are, I tell myself, sympathetically related to the approach taken in John Kerrigan's *Archipelagic English* (2008) and in Andrew McNeillie's country-loving journal *Archipelago*. Kerrigan's book deals with the literature of the 17th century, and with the countrysides – hostile, independent, while also interactive, exquisitely mutual – which became Britain and the home ground of the British Empire, and were drawn into Anglocentricity. Anglo-Welsh Henry Vaughan and Anglo-Scottish William Drummond of Hawthornden are strongly featured.

Another recent book which I have taken to heart is Richard Mabey's *Nature Cure* of 2005, in which the natural world is marvellously pictured, and the arrogance of humanity's exceptionalism restated. There are pictures of the writer's meeting with a fox in the East Anglian wild, and of his totemic, utterly aerial swifts. These pictures constitute his book, or so you might think if it weren't for its abundance of clear statements and wise sayings. Mabey is a naturalist who believes in sentiment, and in a kinship between nature and culture, the non-human and the human. One of his sayings – and of Edward Thompson's before him – states the fallacy: 'man here and nature there.'[23]

I am indebted to Peter Singer's writings on animal liberation, which have made me a belated (fish-eating) vegetarian; to eloquent Tim Dee for his bird watches; and to J.O. Morgan's *Natural Mechanical*, a poem of 2009 in which a boy's encounters with the isle of Skye give proof, if proof were needed, of what the natural world continues to do for the page. From a tree, 'Natureboy', as he is christened in Skye, watches a fox entering a stream with a ball of wool in its snout, gathered from pieces snagged from sheep on a stretch of barbed wire. The fox submerges and vanishes. The ball floats off. And the boy is aware

> That on that small island of wool
> Go teeming and crawling and jumping
> All of the fleas that before were on the fox.

The episode reveals a fox less human but no less crafty than those in the fables set to verse by Robert Henryson in 15th-century Fife, verse which Seamus Heaney has now modernised.[24]

I had almost completed this book when *At the Bright Hem of God* by Peter Conradi was published, a tender account of what was once Radnorshire, of its borderline, bilingual history, of its inhabitants, incomers, eccentric loners. His writers include Henry Vaughan (in Welsh, Fychan), Francis Kilvert, and the Bruce Chatwin of *On the Black Hill* (1982), a self-conscious country book set in the Anglo-Welsh Borderland, a religiously-inclined pastoral romance. Conradi is a part-time countryman who is also a country patriot; he sees himself as savouring what his incomer's presence dilutes. He swears by 'inwardness' and a 'kindly slowness',[25] and he admires this novel of Chatwin's. A certain reserve can be caught in his reference to a review of mine which described the novel as 'a *tour de force* of doorstep exoticism', and as failing in respect of the religious meanings it seeks to express. 'The country is better than the town,' according to my account of the book, 'but the country is terrible. Where, if not in Heaven, are we to live?' Others thought differently, and the novel can be placed with the successful country books of the later last century, along with Laurie Lee's *Cider with Rosie* (1959).

These are pastoral works which can readily be thought to invite you to an elsewhere, to a place quite unlike the one you are in which is also a former place: in each one the action originates at the time of the Great War. Both are verbally and vegetably luxuriant, all but tropical at times, rife with lists and litanies. In each one, country is the real show if not the leading character. Each is exotic and nostalgic. Neither shows a Garden of Eden. But for all the hard times assigned by Chatwin to his innocent male twins, the country matters very much, and much of the trouble is caused by townees. In Laurie Lee's overwritten, taxingly colourful bravura book, an innocent-eye crisis and delirium ascribed to a bygone, 'feudal' age, country matters

matter mightily, and townees are rarely to be seen. Lee's remembered Cotswold place may have reminded its early readers of
the raptures inspired by Dylan Thomas's Fern Hill in his fine
Carmarthenshire poem of the same post-war time, with its
green and golden child, 'famous among the barns', its farm
now 'forever fled'. Lee's green and gold are accompanied by
scabbed schoolboy knees and threadless cotton reels, deployed
as toys – these, too, are a rapturous recall for the right reader.
His place was over the hills but hardly far away from
Radnorshire, and it might perhaps have waited a while. It
would have made a star turn for the Hay-on-Wye Festival.

One of the later chapters of this book speaks of an individual's
double life that takes in town and country. It's about an edition
of the letters of Scotland's Henry Cockburn (1779–1854), historian,
lawyer and country-lover, who lived at a time when a judge
could retire to his 'paradise', as a townsman's country house was
sometimes called, for months of the year, to be with his calves
and his waterfall. I am indebted to James Fergusson for the information that Cockburn took part in the defence of his school
friend, Fergusson's ancestor Patrick Sellar, often denounced as
the principal villain of the Highland Clearances, who was tried
for homicide as a result of his activities as an evicter, and acquitted.
The poor were being piped abroad, from one countryside to
another, that sheep might safely graze.

The rural essays in this book reached a point of mutual
recognition, the perception of a common subject, in the course
of their appearance in journal form. Corrections and the
occasional textual adjustment have been made to the book's
previously published pieces, which appeared without footnotes:
a few have been added here. Some pages bear the hoofprints

of rural rides performed with Seamus Heaney and Andrew O'Hagan. I am grateful to my fellow Celts for their company.

Andrew was later to publish a picaresque Aesopian fable, as told by Marilyn Monroe's dog 'Maf', an urbane creature, and an urban one. For all its animals, this is not a country book, but is nonetheless a version of pastoral. Its living portrait of Maf's 'fated companion', and its experience of Fifties America (O my Lionel and Diana Trilling, and O my infuriated Frank Sinatra), are of their time – the time of writing, the approach to 2010 – while also making use of an ancient topos and tactic.

Andrew, I might mention, comes, as did my grandfather Robert Connor, from the Irvine area of Ayrshire. Backs turned on Ireland produced us both, both Andy and myself.

2

FROM THE LONE SHIELING

'The Canadian Boat Song' was not written by a Canadian. It is a poem of exile, which expresses the sorrow of those who suffered as a result of the Clearances, of the expulsion of crofters from the Highlands and islands of Scotland which began in the later 18th century and went on for a hundred years. But it appears to be the work neither of a Canadian nor of a Scottish Highlander. It has been attributed to city-dwelling D.M. Moir, who was a contributor to *Blackwood's Magazine*, where the poem appeared in their serial symposium, the 'Noctes Ambrosianae', in September 1829. It has also been attributed to John Gibson Lockhart, Walter Scott's biographer and a condemner of the Clearances.

The poem was introduced by the pseudonymous 'Christopher North' (John Wilson) with the explanation that it had come to them together with a letter 'from a friend of mine now in Upper Canada. He was rowed down the St. Lawrence lately, for several days on end, by a set of strapping fellows, all born in that country, and yet hardly one of whom could speak a word of any tongue but the Gaelic.' The poem was described as a translation of one of their songs. As for the friend, he seems to have been the novelist John Galt, at that time a colonial ruler of Upper Canada, who was a friend of Moir's.

Some of the poem is beautiful, and has remained memorable:

> From the lone shieling of the misty island
> Mountains divide us, and the waste of seas –
> Yet still the blood is strong, the heart is Highland,
> And we in dreams behold the Hebrides.

A letter of Lockhart's, from Inverness, indicates that these lines may have been known to him in 1821: 'The room is cold, my hand shakes, the pen is Highland.'

Children had been banished, the poem says, 'that a degenerate Lord might boast his sheep.' In came these lucrative sheep. Out went his smallholders, his crofters. A Hebridean schoolteacher of mine in Edinburgh, Hector MacIver, a gifted and sophisticated man, was, I felt, so moved by the poem that he had to convey that he couldn't abide its outsider's romantic sentimentality, though he could abide, and would recite, Wordsworth's poem about the solitary Highland girl, singing and reaping in the harvest field. His ancestors had been ousted from Uig in the Hebrides, in the 1850s, by 'one of the most humane of Highland landlords', he'd been told, who was just following the fashion for eviction. It seems that they took away with them in their boat the rafters of their house.

The 'plaintive numbers' heard from the Highland girl can be heard again in 'The Canadian Boat Song', whose tears are tribal, but whose mysterious textual history might suggest that nationality is the mother of complication. As in my own case, that of someone who is Scottish and Irish and British. The Scots have recently devolved themselves, though they have yet to desist from electing people to the Westminster Parliament; and there are Scots who wish to separate from England and be their own nation – themselves alone. That would, in my view, be a wrong move rooted in a phobic tribalism, an atavistic and ahistorical tribalism, moreover. The Scots have never been one nation, but always at least two. Scotland, Wales and England share an island, and have run as a not intractable union, *e pluribus*, for three hundred years.

The Highland North-West of Scotland, still residually Gaelic-speaking, has been culturally very different from the Lowlands, whether urban or rural. Hector MacIver had as much trouble speaking the Scots of Robert Burns as Noël Coward would have had. Highlanders were strange when I was young in Edinburgh, their Gaelic speech far stranger than French or German. They were 'clannish'. My family used to refer to my sophisticated teacher as 'the cheuchter', an ugly word of Gaelic origin which meant a rustic or a hick. Since they were half-Irish, they might have seen themselves as not wholly alien to the Hebridean sector of the Gaeltacht – the Celtic common culture which had once spanned the Irish Sea. But they didn't. As I grew up, I grew to be interested in the Irish writers of the modern world, while repelled by the style or movement known as the Celtic Twilight.

This account is not offered as a way of staking a claim to write about the fiction of Alistair MacLeod, in which 'The Canadian Boat Song' has a place. Since I started to read him, his fiction has been widely welcomed in Canada and in America, and he is read in Britain too; and most of his readers in all three countries must feel no less implicated than I am in the tribal or national significance of what he does. He is a Canadian of Scottish–Gaelic-speaking stock whose forefathers settled with compatriots on Cape Breton Island, a northern region of Nova Scotia, early in the 19th century. His fiction tells how these compatriots have since sent sons and daughters down the Atlantic sea coast to the south, throughout the North American hinterlands, and as far afield as mines blasted from the bowels of South Africa.

His first story, 'The Boat', was published in 1968 in the *Massachusetts Review*. Having worked as a teacher, logger and miner, he took to teaching literature and creative writing at the University of Windsor, Ontario. He is the author of sixteen stories – which appeared in two collections later amalgamated and chronologically arranged in a third, *Island* – and of a novel, *No Great Mischief*, which appeared in 2000. His writings are concerned with the clannishness of the old country and of the new one to which this has been transferred, with a hostility towards city life, with the activities of boys, parents, the old, with the sexual lives of strapping fellows and old fellows, and of animals, with the ice that surrounds his island and some small island offshore. The ice grips and relaxes. It joins and it sunders the two islands. It can be walked over, sleighed over. It is good at drowning you. A moving episode in the novel has parents and their boy crossing the ice at night, with lights. One single, stationary light is suddenly seen from the opposite shore.

The deaths described in this heart-shaking passage represent a pivotal point in the dynastic history evident in his fiction. The passage captures MacLeod's sense of a way of life wrung from hardship, expedient, danger and disaster. His books are elemental and ancient. They go back to the world of Odysseus, to Homer's Ithaca. They tell you what his people have to do in order to survive, how they catch fish, fight or sit drinking. And these people do all this without being made to seem simple or naïve, or like specialists in survival.

The clan in the novel is a sept of the MacDonalds – as who should say, the MacLeods. I said to him, when I met him once, that I'd been reading an intriguing account of a 19th-century MacLeod, only to be told by him that there were lots of different MacLeods in the world; he may have thought I was some more than usually flittermouse publicist come to ingratiate myself, who needed to be made aware that a clan was a serious business. But then I knew that already from his books.

The narrator of the novel – the *'ille bhig ruaidh*, or little red boy – is a survivor from the disaster of the drowning, together with his brother Calum, a key dynast and a drinker. In the course of a call home from a uranium mine on the Canadian Shield, the narrator talks to his Grandpa, a man of the senses, a comic foil to the grandparent known to the book in his austerity as Grandfather. Grandpa gives the narrator the customary admonitions on the subject of clan solidarity, fortified with a quotation from 'The Boat Song', from 'that poem your grandfather is always quoting: "Yet still the blood is strong, the heart is Highland." I hope you remember that.' 'Yes,' replies the narrator, a man of few conversational words. 'I remember that.' Grandpa says what Robert the Bruce, the hammer of the English, is supposed to have said at the battle of Bannockburn in 1314, Scotland's favourite date: 'My hope is constant in thee, Clan Donald.' Grandma comes on the line to teach some more lessons: 'Blood is thicker than water, as you've heard us say.' Yes, he has.

Kinship comes first. Duty is important, and is bound up with kinship. It is important to be stoical. The narrator of 'The Boat' provides a portrait of his father, a fisherman opposed by his bitter wife. Eventually there's this: 'And then there came into my heart a very great love for my father and I thought it was very much braver to spend a life doing what you really do not want rather than selfishly following forever your own dreams and inclinations.' To drink is to care, runs a further suggestion – to care about family, and because of it.

That poem is mentioned again in another story, which speaks of the 'stretches of mountain and water' that may lie between relatives and 'those they love'. They lie between these Nova Scotian families and the shielings of their ancestors. Gaels love those they love, it can seem here, and the bardic poetry of the Celtic past is full of how much they hate their enemies, many of them Gaels. They are not ecumenical. They are not multicultural.

A sharp sense of this is felt in 'The Return', which recounts a family visit to a mining town in Cape Breton by an exogamous lawyer from Montreal, his rich wife, and his young son, who tells the story. As they change trains on the island, a blond youth is noticed singing-drunk, and is hurried past by the wife. They are then brought before the tribunal of their not very forbearing ancestors. The son's tall, white-haired granny, smelling of soap and water and hot rolls, casts up her own son's turning-out of his alcoholic brother from his Montreal mansion. Her son defends himself; 'If I were by myself he could have stayed forever.' There's a hint that he might prefer this to what he has – that he might prefer to care for his alcoholic brother. (Care for such a brother, for Calum, is the situation from which *No Great Mischief* unfolds.) Very softly, his mother rejoins:

> But it seems that we can only stay forever if we stay right here. As we have already stayed to the seventh generation. Because in the end that is all there is – just staying. I have lost three children at birth but I've raised eight sons. I have one a lawyer and one a doctor who committed suicide, one who died in coal beneath the sea and one who is a drunkard and four who still work the coal like their father and those four are all that I have that stand by me. It is these four that carry their father now that he needs it, and it is these that carry the drunkard, that dug two days for Andrew's body and that have given me thirty grandchildren in my old age.

There's a 'just staying forever' in this endlessness of 'and's'. MacLeod can seem shy of commas.

Such is the granny's stand against the axiomatically bad outside world, against the daughter-in-law of the corporate lifestyle, to which her lost son the lawyer is literally wedded. MacLeod gives her very good tunes – very good, if at moments magniloquently Biblical, condemnations and dirges. But it would be wrong to decide that the story lacks a sense of what is quenching and constraining in her fanatical insistence.

In 'The Tuning of Perfection' is a righteous old man, Archibald, a widower whose early loss bereaves him for life, whose house sits on a high hill overlooking the sea, on the site of his family's original settlement, and who is a singer of the old Gaelic songs as he believes they have always been sung. He and a coil of relations are invited to take part in a televised folk festival, whose ear-ringed producer, one of the new men, wants their songs cut, in order to stave off boredom. Archibald removes the group from the festival. 'He thought of the impossibility of trimming the songs and of changing them and he wondered why he seemed the only one in his group who harboured such concerns.' The spot goes to a rival group led by the scarred and wily Carver.

The old man is now alone on his high place, sequestered in a style not far from the no-surrender family of anti-statists, holed up in the American West, who lost a son to their besiegers not long ago. He hears a car and prepares to defend himself, measuring his distance in the kitchen from a poker, which he hefts as if it were an 'ancient sword'. His visitors are Carver and his mates, fresh from a car-park scrap, who want to make peace with the old man. Archibald is not mocked in the story, while seeming a little far-out. Hanging on to the old songs is seen as understandable, and more.

Where there's a clan, there's an enemy, and the enemy, in MacLeod's fiction, is the city, with its affluence, its television producers, its publicists, its no time for long songs, its intolerance of drunken relatives. The narrator of *No Great Mischief* embraces the guilty role of a society dentist who had once been down the mines and on Cape Breton's braes. The risk MacLeod has run, as a writer, is that of yielding to the paranoia of the tribe and the special pleading of the tribe, of the small tribe of kin and clan and the larger one of expatriate

Gaeldom. It's a risk against which he succeeds in guarding himself.

His pictures of a collective and individual humanity are among the finest literary achievements of their time, a finer achievement than many currently famous, a relief from the novel of soliloquy which has been in favour, with its reluctance to dramatise and to get out of the author into other people. The lives he describes are more patient, but no narrower, than other lives. He is on their side, but doesn't portray a chosen people, or point to a political programme. He knows the days of a spoken Gaelic may be numbered, but his books bear witness to the survival of the Gaelic tradition: there are colleges devoted to Celtic studies – a new one on the island of Skye, for instance – after the long years of proscription.

The patience of Highlanders, fierce fighters as they have been, has exposed them to exploitation, from the second Jacobite rebellion to the First World War; they fought for their enemies, for their Hanoverian victors, their exploiting chiefs, in regiments raised by local gentries. Few of them had much at stake in the Great War of 1914 (1314 might have been different), where once again it was no great mischief if they fell – which, as the novel explains, is what General Wolfe said of the Highlanders who stormed the heights of Abraham for him against the French.

On both sides of the Atlantic, MacLeod's fiction might possibly be used to make the separatist or devolutionary case from which his fiction refrains. Perhaps there's a risk here too. Not long ago, in Edinburgh, Gore Vidal was heard singing the praises of small nations, having shortly before been singing those of the Oklahoma bomber Timothy McVeigh – of the

Clan or Klan McVeigh, one might add, with an eye on Walter Scott's gift of fiery crosses and other feudal customs to the American South. McVeigh's action was in some degree tribal, in some degree a secession, a declaration of independence. And it was a reminder that small nations have their tribal antecedents and characteristics, and that they have their faults. Guess what would have happened to its black population if the American South had managed to secede. There seems no likelihood of a Nova Scotia *libre*, of a tribal state there of the kind that continues to come about. Strikingly, there's not a word in these books about the politics of Canada: it's as if MacLeod's Highlanders have lived separate lives in that respect, for all their exposure to urban and foreign environments. Tribe, though, is mostly family in his fictions, and the conception of family to be found in them is some distance from the tribalism encountered among modern political parties, as the remains of an old story.

The enemy in MacLeod's fiction has a complex history, which begins with Bonny Prince Charlie and the Forty-Five rebellion, when some of the clans rose in support of a Stuart invasion of Hanoverian Britain, charged and looted their way down to England, turned back towards their glens, and suffered under 'Butcher' Cumberland at the battle of Culloden, and under the persecution that ensued. The attempt to impose a divine-right-of-kings, foreign-faith despotism on a country largely averse to it had failed. MacLeod is not a Jacobite. His Charlie is not the 'unfortunate Prince' of literature and legend. He is under no illusions about the leaders whom his Highlanders served in 1745, or thirteen years later, when they fought bravely for King George, under their old enemy, Wolfe.

The Clearances started to spread with the pacification of the Highlands after Culloden. These are hardly 'old, unhappy, far-off things', a battle long ago: the horror of this dispossession is at the present day an unexpired sentiment, if not a visceral emotion. The dispossession is everywhere in MacLeod's writings. His novel describes the arrival on Cape Breton of the forced-out founder of its expatriate dynasty.

A guide to this Fall from Eden was supplied in 1990 by David Craig with his excellent book, *On the Crofters' Trail*, where he plays the part of an Old Mortality, in search of the Clearance Highlanders and of their descendants in Scotland and in Canada. Alistair MacLeod is shown summering in Inverness County, Cape Breton, among family and friends, and off with the writer to the 'demonic' Hiberno-Scottish fiddle music of a country dance. Craig spells out a memorial on a pile of shingle stones.

PIONEER
DONALD MACLEOD
HIS WIFE
JANET MACPHERSON
APPLIED FOR
AND GRANTED 1808–11
A SECTION OF
THIS THE GOOD EARTH
TRADITION AND
CULTURE ENRICHED
THE LAND OF
THEIR ADOPTION

Craig has a rare eye for northern landscape, for the wild place and the cultivated place, for the very last sweet spot left behind by the cleared Highlanders. This is an essential skill, given his subject. 'Stags were roaring from the slopes of Beinn Dubhain in the damson-dark October gloaming': the prose is richer than MacLeod's, and there may be those for whom the note of threnody and outrage recurs too often. But it's a book that embarrasses such objections.[26]

Poor agricultural land, a rising population – economic historians have argued that the traditional Highland economy was doomed, and that innovation, 'improvement' and dispersal had to happen. But there did not have to be the dispersal that took place. Chiefs became landlords and investors, and legally unprotected tenants were treated with widespread and prolonged brutality, which has been seen by many Scots as Holocaust-like. Clan values never recovered in Scotland. 'The real chieftains were no more,' wrote one observer in the last year of the 19th century; clansmen had refused to join in the game of imitation chieftainship. The clans regrouped, and made a life in various new worlds, where the heart was Highland, where there was hardship, but where there was no feudal lordship. Among the destinations for the country's unwanted at that time was Australia, whose government now turns away boatloads of refugees from terror.

The story 'Vision' (1986) gathers up MacLeod's main concerns. He is attached to an aesthetic in which one story gives rise to another; that is what stories are like, he believes. So 'Vision' is three stories or more. And it has two Cannas: one a Scottish Western Isle, and one in Nova Scotia. At the start of the story a father points out the second of these places,

with its green hills. 'Yes,' says his son. 'I see it. There it is.'
At an earlier point two boys, brothers, one of them this father,
have gone to their Canna to visit grandparents, who are hard
to find. They are diverted to a certain bleak house:

> Framed in the doorway was a tall old woman clad in layers
> of clothing, even though it was summer, and wearing wire-
> framed glasses. On either side of her were two black dogs.
> They were like collies, though they had no white markings . . .
> The boys would have run away but they were afraid that if
> they moved, the dogs would be upon them, so they stayed
> where they were as still as could be. The only sound was the
> tense growling of the dogs. '*Có a th'ann?*' she said in Gaelic.
> 'Who's there?'

The boys leave this tall old woman, who is blind, and the
next thing they experience is the sight of their grandfather
masturbating in his barn. His wife is kind to the boys, frosty
to the onanist. Gradually the lives of the three old people are
unforgettably laid bare.

Their grandfather tells the boys about the original Canna,
and about second-sighted Saint Columba, whose chapel was
on the island, and who grieved for a departure from Ireland:

> Early and late my lamentation,
> Alas, the journey I am making;
> This will be my secret bye-name
> 'Back turned on Ireland'.

The old man proves to have been an illegitimate child who

grew up to become a rider of stallions, and a stallion himself, the lover of the blind woman and of other women. He had been known as Mac an Amharuis, Son of Uncertainty. The boys learn this at a tribunal where they are seeking to enlist in the Great War. They enlist. One loses a leg. The other – the man on the boat who was later to point out the green hills of Canna – is blinded in the Second World War. The story ends with one of MacLeod's knockdown inter-clan fights, in the Legion Hall frequented by veterans.

This is a story about sight and the loss of sight, a theme which seems related to a preoccupation with the power of sexual passion and with its dark outcomes. These include, in this case, the uncertainties of a dynastic succession. There may be an air of contrivance to the way in which the observant fisherman of the opening pages is only later discovered to be blind. A small difficulty, this – comparable, perhaps, as one of MacLeod's few possible aberrations, to the discovery by the family in the novel that their house has been set on fire. By one of the French Canadians with whom the MacDonalds are at feud? The arsonists are never identified, and the subject is dropped.

MacLeod likes to write about sexual activity. Even his old men are sexually unspent – a state, I notice, for which writers seldom have much time. Husbands and wives do it, and other people too. Animals do it. A cow moans and bawls her passion from the barn, till the day arrives when the farmer helps a bull's penis into her with his own large hand. Bulls advance snorting and drooling with lust. Eagle mates are tender and companionate. When the comic grandfather in *No Great Mischief* returned to Cape Breton in his youth, he used to get

an erection at the very sight of the island. In these fictions is
an *Amor vincit omnia* which is neither fanciful nor exhibi-
tionist. It is all true. Passion is duly awarded its exhaustions
and its dark and cursing outcomes.

The animals in the books are as clannish as the dynasties
are, as loyal to their human beings as the human beings are
to their kinsfolk, and, without being in the least anthropo-
morphised, as much of a living presence, almost every one of
them an individual. The story of the mother dog who leaps
on her old master to lick his face, and thereby excites her sons
to tear his throat out, has great resonance. When, elsewhere,
a lighthouse-keeper's daughter rises in the night to go to the
neighbouring shanties to make love with a distant relative,
soon to die in a logging accident in Maine, we are told more
about the body of the dog by her bed than we are about the
man's. 'The eyes of the dog seemed to glow in the dark and
she felt the cold wetness of its nose when she extended her
hand beyond the boundary of the bed. She could smell the
wetness of its coat, and when she moved her hand across its
head and down its neck the water filmed upon her palm.'
What goes on in the shanty is nevertheless perfectly in focus.
She spends the rest of her life as a keeper of the light until
the Government automates it. On one occasion she is taken
sexually by some fisherman; no word of blame, no comment
indeed, is expressed. Then she disappears from the world of
her relatives.

Alistair MacLeod must be doing all right: slurs have started
to appear. I have seen a letter in a newspaper reproaching him
for a geographical error in the return visit to Scotland that
occurs in his novel. He has also been complained of for

producing an ambience of males: it seems clear to me that his tall old women are even more important to his fiction than his old men. One important woman, a widow of long standing, is dying on her farm at Rankin's Point, and is visited by a grandson, Calum, also dying, his blood 'diseased'. Her husband's blood is still remembered, as it stained the road to the farm, many years before. Her blood relations press her to enter a nursing home, but she wants to tough it out at Rankin's Point, until she is found dead on the same road by Calum, after a family reunion with jigs and reels, where the fiddle is played in the old way, but where the young ones have brought guitars. Here is a tribal intransigence, tracked by death, and encircled by later generations who haven't deserted her but in whom the Highland blood may no longer be as strong as it was once. The scene reminds me of a Celtic dream I have had, in which an aunt of mine dies on her own in an ancient shieling, on a hill.

I am writing this in Brittany, where there's a place named Gael and an Inter-Celtic festival is advertised with a harp-hefting poster. The Breton language is a form of Gaelic, and a million Bretons are said to speak it. In a nearby village, ten families each lost three or more sons in the war of 1914 – another case of 'no great mischief'. Then, in the castled town of Josselin, I came across a pair of young women playing the flute and the accordion beside the church door, with a casket at their feet for francs. I was overcome with joy. Very good musicians they were, and they were very good musicians for hours on end, with no song heard more than once. Sarah and Rachel, Jewish perhaps, have the memories of Early Modern Scottish ballad-reciters. The group is called by a Breton name,

Kan Ha Distroy, and their songs are presented as Breton and as *traditionelles*. They are, in fact, from all over the complicated Celtic diaspora: there were Scottish, Irish and French Canadian songs that day, as well as French.

MacLeod's singers are not remote from these memorious young women. These women don't sound nostalgic. They sell tapes of their music, and may perhaps trim some of their songs. It may be that, unlike Archibald, his old Gaelic singer, they belong to the media. At the same time, they are enabling a civilisation to survive, even if its old language is to cease to be a vernacular. Alistair MacLeod is doing this too. I hope he would see them as sisters.

3

MCGAHERN'S HARD SAYINGS

At John McGahern's funeral in the Irish countryside the Catholic hierarchy was in attendance. For one observer, there was the sense of a mild monsignorial jostling, after which a priest stepped forward to express regret for a past mistreatment of the writer at the hands of the Church. McGahern's early fiction was banned in Ireland, and cost him his job as a schoolmaster. Once bitten, once a scandal, he had since become a credit to the community of the faithful.

His novels and stories, and his *Memoir* of 2005, are not such as to persuade many readers that this medieval-seeming penitence – a Canossa in reverse, with its papal amends – has to be thought arbitrary or incongruous. His scenes from clerical life can be bleak and unillusioned. Most of his people lead 'sensible pagan lives'. They tell their beads and go to Mass for reasons of custom and solidarity, rather than doctrine. But the customs and ceremonies of the Church illuminate his books, both literally and figuratively. The parish church stood, 'through the great feasts of Christmas', like 'a lighted ship moored in a sea of darkness'. At the centre of it all is his feeling for his mother, celebrated in his books to the point, for some Irish readers, of Mariolatry.

For the boy Sean McGahern, she was 'my beloved'. She caused him to remember, at the end of his days, that 'our heaven was here in Aughawillan'. She was the Church in person, the part of it that could be loved, and there was the hope that he would one day serve her by becoming a priest. In the novel *Amongst Women* (1991), she turns into the stepmother Rose, who wants everything to move 'towards reconciliation and the unquestioning love she herself felt with her whole heart'. His mother believed that 'God is great' and that 'God knows best,' while his fiction is apt to suggest that human beings 'know nothing'. She believed that God had taken away her health in order to test her faith. Her death from cancer, at the age of forty-two, occasions, in the memoir, a *Liebestod* of marked intensity. Her son was later to leave the Church, but was never to leave his mother.

McGahern's art has its own ceremonies. It takes pleasure in regularity and in repetition; it has some striking duplications. It travels with the seasons and the sun and moon. His is a plain style of the utmost directness, charged with vigilance and subtlety. The journey to school of the boy and his mother, with its serial Mahons, is recited like a doxology in the memoir – 'past Brady's house and pool and the house where the old Mahon brothers lived, past the deep, dark quarry and across the railway bridge and up the hill by Mahon's shop' – just as, in the writings at large, the same story, his own, is told and retold.

The paradise of his childhood was subject to expulsions. His father, a policeman, with his uniform's three silver stripes, was darker than any quarry, a restless bully, a beater of his children. 'The hard way is the only way,' says the father he invents for one of his stories. When his real father claims in the memoir to be missing his dead wife, the boy 'knew that he was lying . . . though I would have given the whole world for the mercy of the picture he painted'. It was as bad as that. His father passes through several incarnations in the writings, and is at his worst in the last judgement delivered in the memoir. The patriarch Moran in *Amongst Women* is assigned a charm that is more apparent, at times, to his oppressed womenfolk than it is likely to be to the reader. His children resort to subterfuge and to outright rebellion, but his will, his hard way, persists to the end on the home ground of the farm. The various images and analogues of his father in McGahern's fiction leave an impression both of the uniqueness and uncertainty of the individual self and of his father's affinity with others in the society, those who are the same but different, like and unlike the Sergeant of Cootehall.

'Help them,' advises an old drinking dominie in the story 'High Ground': 'Women are weak.' They do need help in McGahern's fiction, and are many times refused it. From weak to wilful, virgin mother to virago, women are a suitably wide spectrum, and a crucial presence, in the Ireland of his books, where they are also seen to be in a state of subjection. The 'unquestioning love' ascribed to the stepmother Rose might seem to risk sentimentality. But he is rarely a sentimental writer, and Rose is awarded, elsewhere in his fiction, a hostility to the husband she bears and manages and can even be charmed by in *Amongst Women*. McGahern is often austere. And yet he is notably affectionate about the people he creates and commemorates, his 'creatures of the earth', and is persuasive about the good he finds there. Their tea with buttered bread is a feast.

We are mostly in the West, in Leitrim or Roscommon, in a small place where 'nothing much ever happened', as he is given to saying, and where much does happen, rather as his womenfolk are at once subordinate and important. Here is the barracks where his father rules, with the mother away with her children on a farm, or else in hospital. Near his different dwellings are healing waters – a river and a lake. Near, too, is the great Gloria Bog.

McGahern's art is derived, early and late, from his experiences as a son. Dating from the 1970s, the stories which can now be read in a selection, *Creatures of the Earth*[27] – drawn from the revised *Collected Stories* of 1992, with the inclusion of two new items – ushered in the experiences of a man among women. Sexual intercourse begins. 'A meal of each other's flesh' follows fast on encounters in dance halls. 'Love flies out the window,' as he is also given to saying, and as it does in his outstanding story 'My Love, My Umbrella', where the self-centred teller of the tale comes to grief. In his novel of 1979, *The Pornographer*, another selfish narrator lords it over two successive women. By now he is making use of urban settings – of Dublin and London. His Irish countryside has its stock of 'been-to's', in the Indian phrase, of men and women who have been to the fair cities of England and America, in search of a living and in danger of losing the native gentleness of their manners.

In an obituary tribute Colm Tóibín told how, at a literary conference where writers were urged to display political commitment, McGahern spoke up in dissent: 'It is a writer's job to look after his sentences. Nothing else.' Can he have meant this pastoral injunction? The 'war that was still raging in Europe' gets no more attention in his novels and stories than the Napoleonic struggle does in Jane Austen. But Ireland's wars are in evidence. His father belonged to the IRA, and one of his fictional fathers is shown in action against the Black and Tans. In *That They May Face the Rising Sun* (2002), a local IRA worthy, a former prisoner of the British, is quietly opposed by the novel's main man, Joe Ruttledge, who has returned from London with his wife Kate (in the manner of McGahern himself). Ruttledge remarks that the country is already free. 'Not all of it,' replies the respected citizen, no less quietly.

Throughout his work a sense of the Irish locality as something other than a small place carved on its piece of ivory is clearly registered. In the novella *The Leavetaking* (1975), a teacher is sacked for marrying without the sanction of the Church: it's a 'crazy country', he reflects, which fires people for such reasons. Crazily, too, his real father threatens his little ones with 'I'll pack you all off to the orphanage where the nuns and brothers won't be long in bringing you to your senses.' And the Ireland that ensued on the Second World War is condemned, in *Amongst Women*, by a veteran freedom fighter, as 'the mixture of druids and crooks that we're stuck with', which earns the indignation of his old comrade, the patriarch Moran. The memoir is stoical, but firmly critical, in its discussions of the bygone Irish theocracy.

The collection of 1985, *High Ground*, reveals an urban Ireland explored by a young man from the country. 'Bank Holiday' is a romance gargoyled by Dublin's literati, who also figure in 'Parachutes', where love flies out the window and the narrator is left with the geniuses in their pub. 'High Ground', the title story, describes a Haugheyesque politico: such men are now a higher power in the countryside than the priest who used to run the school and much of the community. 'The Conversion of William Kirkwood' studies a benign, eccentric, once-Protestant landowner. McGahern has a kindness for lairds, as for labourers: two of his best pieces relate to British building sites and their guest workers. The hostile father appears in *High Ground*'s 'The Gold Watch', together with the step-mother Rose of *Amongst Women*. The closing passages of the story have been reworded, as part of a process of trimming and repunctuation which the stories have undergone since they were first published, but the meaning of these closing passages remains at certain points elusive. A summarising eloquence of his, touching on 'the nature of things', can some-times give, as here, a sense of strain.

McGahern's gift for the short story is fully apparent in the new stories included in *Creatures of the Earth*. The title story has a retired doctor and his wife who find they are 'no longer useful', and are dropped by friends and colleagues. The wife becomes a widow and retires to a lonely place, her only friend a daughter soon to marry. Two pets are successively killed by different males – an unsettling duplication. Old Ireland has changed with the change of life experienced by the couple. Authority is gone. Priest and doctor are disbelieved. 'Mere anarchy' takes the form of a human meanness polluting a beautifully rendered cliffscape.

The other new story, powerfully dramatised, speaks of neigh-bourhood spies who also complain that the country has changed. You no longer lie on the bed you have made. Couples separate, commit adultery. Kate Ruttledge is a reader – an activity seldom predicated now of fictional characters – and would be well on the way to divorce had she lived in London or Luton. 'The blackbirds and thrushes racketed. A robin sang. Maggie was still there, praise be to everything that moves or sings.' The birds are a mantra of the story, which gives way here to an affirmation of Kate's love for her mother.

One of McGahern's favourite writers was the Scottish-Canadian Alistair MacLeod. Both bring something quite distinctive, something ancient, to the operations of a prevailing metropolitan culture. In both cases, the richness of manual labour is evoked by someone who has bent his back. Birds, animals, plants, weather are never incidental or decorative. They matter, rather as the people do. McGahern's country place is no paradise lost, and few of his urban readers can have felt that they were being enlisted in a version of pastoral. He has lived, and is known, in cities, has been read and recognised in France. Tóibín remarked in his tribute that at one time 'Enniskillen, rather than Dublin, was his capital, and after Enniskillen, Paris.'

Many of his sentences are interestingly sententious. 'Though children are seldom fair, they have a passion for fairness.' There is a moment in the *Nightlines* collection of 1970 when we read about what happens when 'people look to each other for happiness or whatever it is called.' Eight years later, in *Getting Through*, perhaps it is 'better not to have been born at all'. Some of these sentences would appear to deny the happiness recalled in the memoir – the times with his mother, or alone on the river. Some have the ring of his encourager Beckett, on the occasions when Beckett offers his fatalistic bad news about the human condition and its slavery to limit. One or two echo his father's hard sayings. There's a story in *Nightlines* where 'I shouted almost in his voice'.

John McGahern likes to write about darkness, and can sometimes seem to be its friend: 'why should we wish the darkness harm, it is our element; or curse the darkness because we are doomed to love in it, and die . . .' This is from 'Along the Edges', in *Getting Through*. The memoir says about everyone in the world what his embodiment Joe Ruttledge says about his neighbours: 'I suppose they'll move around in the light for a while like the rest of us and disappear.' The darkness Ruttledge has in mind does not seem to allow for the hope of heaven. McGahern's play *The Power of Darkness*, a Leitrimisation of the melodrama by Tolstoy of the same name, proves, surprisingly, to be a very funny Jacobean-bucolic farce, a jig of poisoners round a dying patriarch, in which, once more, 'love flies out the window.'

McGahern's fictions were capped by the memoir, a late work which is at least as satisfying, in its candour and imaginative fervour, as any of his stories. What does art add, in this case, to autobiography? The answer should make room for the thought that the memoir and the variously gifted novels and stories are all of them art. They drink from the same well. They are the one dark, veracious, chiefly country thing.

4

THE PASSION
OF ALICE LAIDLAW

I stood in July 2006 with two other descendants of the rural working class in a country churchyard hidden away in the Scottish Borders. We stood at the grave of a fourth such descendant, the novelist and poet James Hogg, 'the Ettrick Shepherd', author of the *Confessions of a Justified Sinner*, who herded sheep for much of his life and was often referred to as 'poor Hogg'. All four of us count in different degrees as country folk by origin, as does the writer of stories Alice Munro, Hogg's collateral descendant, who says in a new book of hers[28] that her family from the hinterland of Ontario were 'poor people', the sort who are 'burdened with more intelligence than their status gives them credit for'.

Many share this status, and many of them could tell stories, as Munro does, about a denial of credit. Country life is still around, still potent, practically and imaginatively, both in fact and in memory, individual and ancestral. 'We in dreams behold the Hebrides,' and we still live there, too, some of us. And the poor people who live in or hail from the country continue to be known for the books they sometimes write. *Requiescat* John McGahern, who died in 2006 and who grew up and ended his days in the country. Not everyone who lives there resembles the gomerils pictured in sour R.S. Thomas's (fine) poem 'On the Farm'.

You get to Ettrick churchyard by climbing an avenue shaded by tall dark trees keyed to the long sleeps that lie ahead. Ranged round a kirk rebuilt in the 1820s, it's a compact little spot, the locals tightly marshalled. Hogg is interred together with his kin. The grave of his maternal grandfather, the last man in the region to converse with the fairies and an ancestor shared with Alice Munro, carries a lightsome epitaph worded by Hogg: here, grounded, lies 'the far-famed Will o' Phaup, who for feats of frolic, agility and strength had no equal in his day'. Inside, the kirk is as wooden as a cigar box, with the pews dominated from on high by a pulpit that suggests an eagle's spread wings. The Presbyterian minister Thomas Boston was once the eagle of the parish: Calvinist, miserabilist, strong for original sin, famous for his books and sermons. The present incumbent is from what used to be Czechoslovakia, and has raised at least one Ettrick eyebrow by teaching his children Czech.

The friends who stood with me in homage to Hogg and his leaping grandfather were the writers Seamus Heaney and Andrew O'Hagan – Irish, the three of us, or, in Andrew's case and mine, Ir-ish, since we are also Scottish, brought up in Scotland and attached to it (though not 'proud' of it, in the manner expected of patriots). I was brought up as a Presbyterian, while the others are of Catholic stock. We were engaged in the old-fashioned pursuit of driving round the country looking at places of literary interest, the whereabouts, mainly, of Hogg and Robert Burns, such as the bridge where Tam o' Shanter's mare lost her tail to a witch, and Tibbie Shiel's Inn by St Mary's Loch where Hogg was friends with a landlady whose firm views ('Hogg was a gey sensible man, for a' the nonsense he wrat') are almost outdone by the present landlady's, and whose two successive photographs hang on the walls, a handsome face of Bostonian gravity, conscious finally of her coming death.

Andrew's car was as much of a wonder as Will o' Phaup. A satellite-controlled itinerary gleamed on a mini-screen above the dashboard, and a female voice, known to us as Tinkerbell, would tell us, to the yard, in the veriest hamlet, how to rejoin the motorway. Seamus's far fame had reached these parts. At Tibbie Shiel's, a woman came to breakfast with a copy of his poems in her hand; two hours later, at the prehistoric mound of Cairnpapple in central Scotland, from which can be glimpsed the seas on either side, an Irish farmer greeted him and they walked together like country people at a market, I fondly mused.

We told stories in the car, and out of it. Seamus told of a gentleman of the road, motoring in the Highlands, who pulls up at a T-junction. A sign says 'Inverness 25 miles', and another sign, pointing in the opposite direction, says the same. The man addresses a peasant digging nearby: 'Good morning. Does it matter which road I take?' And the other man replies: 'Nae to me, it doesn't.' Nae prizes for guessing which of the parties to this dialogue gained the sympathy of the three travellers. None of us believes that working-class is always best, in the knowledge that it's widely seen as something to be disguised or escaped: but we joined in that 'nae to me'. Seamus's poem, one of his first, about watching his father digging came to mind.

Andrew was later to be punished for enjoying this Scottish joke by being clawed at in a Scottish journal for despising his native Ayrshire, if not his native Scotland, and for alleging the presence in the shire of depression and of anti-Catholic and anti-English sentiment; living in London, he was as bad as James Boswell – as it happens, one of Scotland's most interesting writers. The charges were levelled in a review of his novel *Be Near Me*, in which the West of Scotland and the South of England memorably collide. A piece by him, published in 2002, in which a Scottish self-pity and delusion were anatomised, has proved memorable too.

We dined in Edinburgh with the composer James MacMillan, who spoke bravely a few years ago about the time-honoured persecution of Catholics in Scotland and was rewarded by being doorstepped and vilified by newspapermen who wanted to find out if he belonged to Opus Dei. We'd previously paid our respects to an elderly writer, Edwin Morgan, who'd long been troubled, as we subsequently learnt, by a perceived Catholic threat. He seemed to like the sound of the word 'no', and may perhaps have said it of his three visitors once we'd gone.

On returning to London, I discovered that the then Prime Minister, Tony Blair, would be helping the Israeli Government to bomb the Lebanese poor, with a third of the casualties reportedly children. He would soon be explaining to the electorate how pained he was by the tragic loss of life that had come about.

Something else awaited me in London. I received a proof copy of Alice Munro's new collection of stories, *The View from Castle Rock*, which begins in the Ettrick valley with an attention to Will o' Phaup's tombstone and a role for Hogg's cousin James Laidlaw, who left Ettrick for North America at the age of 60 and settled in Ontario, where a descendant begat Alice Munro. The book describes how, on the top of Edinburgh Castle, James had informed his children, in his cups, that to look over to Fife was to behold the shores of America. He is studied with recourse to his letters, which I consulted when I wrote a book about Hogg. He was an opinionated and bigoted fellow and Munro has him down as a shipboard buttonholer. He believed in the justified sinner, and objected to Canada's Methodists for supposing that a man may be justified, accepted by God, 'and fall from it tomorrow', the just being for ever secure. He would have had no time for Catholics. He pities his cousin, 'Hogg, poor man', for spending 'much of his time coining lies' (Alice Munro gives 'conning'). Poor Hogg made things up and got more money for his lies, according to James, than Thomas Boston ever did for his sermons.[29]

Writing, of the literary sort, was unfavourably known as 'making things up' in the Ontario of Alice Laidlaw's girlhood, where pioneer-puritan severities had yet to disappear and the notion of punishment was popular. 'Not just Presbyterians but almost everybody else believed that God rewarded lust with dead babies, idiots, hare-lips and withered limbs and club-feet' (James Hogg's opinion of illegitimate children, of whom he had one and possibly two, could come close to that belief). Munro's account of one of her fictional girls gives a clear indication of what country life could mean for Alice Laidlaw when she began to seem strange to those around her and to call attention to herself and to make things up: 'Her sort of intelligence was often put in the same category as a limp or an extra thumb.' Art, as well as lust, could attract the wrath of God.

Her daughter Sheila says in her book *Lives of Mothers and Daughters*[30] that she has found herself unable to 'unravel the truth of my mother's fiction from the reality of what actually happened'. Writing in the past about Munro's art, I tried to discuss its relation to actuality, pointing out that it uses the facts of her life, a practice of hers that was once a bone of contention for some, but that, for art's sake, these facts are changed, made over, made up indeed, re-imagined. In the foreword to the new collection, which moves from the pioneers to the end of her first marriage, her mother's death and the advent of a stepmother she doesn't get on with, she observes that these stories are different from her other stories by virtue of their relative proximity to the facts of her life. For all that, they are fiction.

> You could say that such stories pay more attention to the truth of a life than fiction usually does. But not enough to swear on. And the part of this book that might be called family history has expanded into fiction, but always within the outline of a true narrative.

This leaves you feeling that these stories are like the others after all, being at once her life and her art. Old questions, including James Laidlaw's, about art's lies and feigning, arise here, as they do elsewhere in the book, when she alludes, cannily enough, to 'canny lying of the sort you can depend upon a writer to do'. Why should art make things up? Why doesn't it stick to the facts? Munro's art is such as to wipe away the tears that may be inherent in such questions. You feel that the changes it makes to the facts of her life are as true as any of the facts could be. The changes are her.

The new stories make use of family papers and public records. She once spent time looking and learning in Selkirkshire, with its heritage of battles and ballads and the spirits of the glen. There were those in her earlier life who thought that writing meant handwriting; her stepmother assured her that her father wrote better than her – in that sense, as she then gathered. But he was also a writer in the other sense: late in life, after his years as a fox farmer and nightwatchman, he wrote about the pioneer life of his forebears, and he was not the only family member who could, in that sense, write. The diary of young Walter Laidlaw, James's son, lends quotations here. The archives offered her plenty of stuff to incorporate and supplement, including items unfamiliar to me as a biographer of Hogg. The high house of Phaup, up in the hills above Ettrick kirk, near the burial-place of Hogg's sinner, is said to be the place where Hogg's shepherd friends met for debates and were held to have caused the disastrous storm of 1794 by trying to raise the Devil. This is the region where the Ettrick and the Yarrow start their streams, purling down towards Walter Scott's baronial Abbotsford and the Tweed.

Some of the stories can be matched with stories published previously. They breathe the same air and re-work the same material. An earlier story, 'The Wilderness Station', goes back to the pioneers and shows two of them clearing the ground for their first settlement. With its possible fratricide and unreliable confession, the story has been termed a re-imagining of Hogg's masterpiece.

'I grew older. I became useful around the house. I learned not to give lip. I found ways to make myself agreeable.' Her stories represent her as vulnerable, and as thought to be difficult. She can be at times like the little pitcher with long ears. Her writing father, to whom she was close, searingly beat her, it seems, an event described and adapted in the past and described and adapted again now. It would be a mistake to underrate the turbulence and profound effect of her adolescent sense of incongruity and rejection, which had in time to make what it could of the impending counter-culture of the 1960s, when shaggy clothes and long hair and a long-presaged liberation reached the prairies. Her daughter relates that Charles Kingsley's injunction used to be talked of in the family as she grew up:

> Be good sweet maid
> And let who will be clever.

And that her mother would recall: 'I thought I'd do the opposite.' Her mother thought that niceness could be 'a terrible abnegation of self'. But she'd also wonder whether the counter-culture might have 'made me self-centred'.

Poetry and poverty and sexual love are leading concerns of the poetry of Burns, and Alice Munro deals with them too. The favourite lines of verse spoken of here as filling her young head led on to the poetry of her stories. Several of them are about menial tasks, and two of the greatest and most affecting, 'Walker Brothers Cowboy' and 'Thanks for the Ride', are about love. In the new collection a girl like her takes up with a broad-shouldered Salvation Army stable boy (the Salvation Army bit is invented), and trysts with him in a hayloft, where the romance suffers a complication. She likes to lie longing on the ground, staring up into the foliage of an apple orchard, and her desire for the boy is made vivid with nothing at all in the way of show or exclamation. Aware of, but not sold on, the hippies of the time, she was never a poet of the counter-culture. She finds a mystery in sexuality, but was never a sex priestess. And the candour and verisimilitude of her treatment of 'lust' have survived long after flower power had shed its petals. The conclusion of the story recalls that 'it was in books that I would find, for the next few years, my lovers. They were men, not boys. They were self-possessed and sardonic, with a ferocious streak in them, reserves of gloom.' Books apart, though, 'it was not as if I had given up on passion. Passion, indeed, whole-hearted, even destructive passion was what I was after. Demand and submission.'

There's a story in the collection, as in a previous collection, in which she visits her father in hospital, where he is dying. She no longer taxes herself, she reflects, with the deep ques-tions – are we right about evolution, and the like – which she used to think about. 'Now I think about my work, and about men.' It is as if she is saying this to severe James Laidlaw of Ettrick.

The story then takes a sharp turn, which points to the breadth of register in her family-oriented fiction. Her step-mother's dog has been constipated, but a break-through is about to occur, in time for a family snack. Her stepmother is overjoyed. 'I can tell by the sound he makes when he's got it worked down into a better position where he can make the effort. There's some pie left, we never finished it, would you rather have the pie?' Alice picks up a ham sandwich.

The collection, which has opened in Ettrick and gone with the pioneers to Illinois and on their great trek north to Ontario, ends with a return to the genealogy of the pioneers and with the authoress up to her ankles in poison ivy as she searches for a forgotten grave. Graves can only do so much, you feel. But this is a rare and fascinating work, in which the past makes sense of the present and the present makes sense of the past, and the two are both a continuum and a divorce. It is very much a memoir, as well as a set of fictions. But then the whole corpus of her stories is a memoir, the novel of her life. It is silly to complain, as some once did, that she writes not novels but stories. The book says barely anything about Hogg's *Confessions*, but it's more than likely that the novel has been an influence on what she has done. She is the cooler, the more deliberate artist of the two, her tales plainer. But they can be drawn all the same to uncertainty. 'When you write about real people you are always up against contradictions.'

My love for her work is touched, in my own eyes, with augury and coincidence. I was born within weeks of her, and am acquainted with the Border lands of her forebears. When I was writing about James Hogg, my thoughts would fasten on the case of that other country writer Alice Munro, and I was later told, in a Cambridge tearoom, that she was a relative of his. I went with my friends to stand at her ancestor's grave and was then handed a book that did the same. Moved by the power, for all its faults, of country life, I am able to think of her, and of my travelling friends and myself, as figures in a pre-industrial landscape, one embodied in the here and now. When the lights are low, I feel that we belong to an archaic world of peasants and spirits, where the people have no more possessions than Lebanese villagers had before the bombs fell, but where they will sometimes write poems and stories.

When Alan Hollinghurst called me Professor Ettrick for a satirical cameo to be found in his recent novel about high life in London, he was referring to a very small, dispersed place, still quite lonely, a far cry from the novel's Notting Hill Gate. Ettrick, though, with its art and ancient bloodshed, its writers and its reivers, has a past which allows you to say that this is a place which has taken part in the minstrelsy of the Scottish Border, in the history and literature of Scotland, and in the making of Canada and of Canadian literature. It is good to think of Alice Munro walking about its absence of streets.

5

EDWARD AND FLORENCE

Tony Blair is said to have mistaken the novelist Ian McEwan for a painter of pictures. To be fair to the prime minister, McEwan's artistic identity is far from straightforward. He is a Dutch-interior realist (in that sense a painter) who is also a romantic fabulist, a specialist in what once was called the 'frightful' and the 'unaccountable' – an old word employed by him in something like the old spirit. He is a springer of shocks and horrors of the sort that electrified the Jacobean stage. He goes in for secrecy and uncertainty, for dual identity, and for often mysterious memorable episodes – among them, the pub scene of filial and primordial *déjà vu* in *The Child in Time* of 1987, which turns out to support the ensuing plot. Some of this can make him look like an entertainer, or a writer of thrillers. But such terms are apt to seem out of place when applied to his writings, which are also, for one thing, those of a learned man, whose accounts of quantum electrodynamics and other arcana have instructed and abashed a generation of literary readers. Novels are not always informative, but McEwan's are.

He is now, at no great age, the author of a body of fiction full of range and change and invention. A new book by him has long been an event. This new book, though, *On Chesil Beach*,[31] is more than an event. It is a masterpiece. The very idea that informs it, fascinating and unfamiliar, is masterly.

Of his novel of 1993, *Black Dogs*, a critic claimed that it was a 'regeneration': it represented 'McEwan's transformation from a purveyor of knowingly nasty tales to a novelist unsurpassed for his responsive, responsible humanity'. This is to speak ill of *The Cement Garden* (1978), his earliest novel and one of his best, which has its element of the macabre and untoward (incest, the hugger-mugger of a premature burial of a kind), but which isn't nasty or inhumane. But it's true that the macabre of the earlier fiction, and the youthfulness that shaped it, are not in evidence here. The new book is shocking, dark, at times. But it has very little of the romantic material of several of the foregoing fictions. It is not fabulous. It is accountable, domestic. It imagines, with humanity, the plight of a severely bashful virgin.

The virgins, Edward and Florence, who are at the heart of this closely focused work were born around 1940, some eight years before their author, and they are at the cusp of a development, an exposure to changing times, which ran in parallel with the youth of Ian McEwan, who went off with the loot from his first published short story and blissed out in Afghanistan. In 1972 he returned to England and got on with an exemplary professional career. He had suffered the Sixties liberations which the experience of his courting couple predates. As in the case of Alice Munro, these liberations are a pivotal matter in McEwan's stories.

Even when they are alone, Edward and Flo are oppressed by 'a thousand unacknowledged rules'. They don't do childish

things: 'being childish was not yet honourable, or in fashion.'
A flower was a thing of beauty – not yet a statement. Ahead
lies the famous decade of 'new excitements and freedoms and
fashions', and a 'chaos of numerous love affairs': an era in
which chaste women (and men) were swept into a preached
and prescribed libertinage, and sweet girl graduates could feel
that they had to oblige.

Too late for Phillip Larkin, as he proclaimed in one of his
poems, sexual intercourse began in 1963, which is about the
time when the option raised its lizard head for Florence. For
her, the words for it are virtually unspeakable, rather as she
finds the word 'cancer'. Flo's debut is to recall that of the
county bride who was reported to have sent a telegram the
morning after her wedding night: 'Coming back immediately.
Johnny's gone mad.'

The novel opens as the pair sit down to dinner, on their
wedding night, at a seaside hotel in Dorset, and it embarks
on a journey to the end of the night, with cunning flash-
backs designed to establish parentage and background: tenses
are kept in control, as they frequently aren't with such
customary interminglings of present and past. This is a tight
ship, moored by Chesil's celebrated shingle beach, no less
important to its novel than is the Cobb at nearby Lyme
Regis to one of Jane Austen's. Florence is 'serious', her bride-
groom rightly thinks; she is blossoming into the first violin
of her own string quartet, very much intent on success and
on the Wigmore Hall. Her father is a brooding presence: a
constraint has fallen on the two, and they don't find it easy
to speak or to stroke. Edward is a strong lad from the Chilterns
– serious too, a historian at the university he attended, yet

a scrapper outside pubs, now set to join his father-in-law's science business.

He is charged with seed-spilling physical desire for Alice-banded Florence, who loves him back, but in her own shy way, a way that grew to be unpopular in the Sixties, in many circles, and thereafter to be left unsung in literary circles, which is one reason why the idea of the book may present itself as original. Novelists acquired a habit of ignoring or disrespecting the fear of physical love. There must have been a lot of that fear still about in later decades, as there no doubt was in the 18th century, when the gifted memorial writer Louisa Stuart[32] held that to come across in books allusions to *l'amour physique* was like being forced into the kitchen and the slaughterhouse when all you wanted was your dinner: but the novelists of the later 20th century were to turn their eyes away from such fears. McEwan respects Flo's visceral reluctance, while also respecting her lover's ill-fated attempts to cope with her shyness and to be forbearing. Much of the book describes – in a Kama Sutra of clumsiness and deferment, told to the last trapped pubic hair – the foreplays that anticipate and accompany their nuptials. The inordinate foreplays of the Fifties.

Edward had known that on a certain date in July 'the most sensitive portion of himself would reside, however briefly, within a naturally formed cavity inside this cheerful, pretty, formidably intelligent woman. How this was to be achieved without absurdity, or disappointment, troubled him.' Florence's trouble was a good deal worse. She did not wish to be 'entered', 'penetrated', as her sex manual had led her to expect. Sex was the price that love had to pay, and falling in love had revealed to her 'just how odd' she was in her dismay. Unlike her liberated girlfriends at the Royal College of Music, 'she felt the peculiar unshared flavour of her own existence: she was alone.' She is wonderfully characterised, as indeed Edward is: she's a decisive leader of the quartet, but 'whenever she was anxious or too self-conscious, her hand would repeatedly rise to her forehead to brush away an imaginary strand of hair, a gentle, fluttering motion that would continue long after the source of stress had vanished.'

What is it to love someone you fear to touch, or be touched by, sexually? What is likely to be in store for such a shyness? What does it stand to lose? These are among the questions asked or adumbrated here.

The novel reaches its climax in the newly-weds' four-poster bed and in the fraught conversation that follows in the twilight of Chesil's shingled beach. This scene is perhaps the greatest of McEwan's memorable episodes, generating an even more forceful and an even finer suspense than any in his writings, and the outcome is all the more impressive for being well-judged and true to life, just as the grisliness of their sexual turmoil is the more impressive for lying within the boundaries of common experience. It's worth adding that the same can often be said of the 'nastiness' once attributed to his earlier fictions. There's a weirdness of the home to be met with in these books, and in this one.

The novel has felicities which ensure, rather than embellish, the humanity of its sense of the lovers' predicament. This appears when Florence, stretched out fearfully in the four-poster, glances up and notices a green stain on the fabric: 'How had that got there?' she thinks to herself. The sight ties in with an earlier stain and looks forward to a possible later one. Is she too to be stained? She is reminded of being with her father in the cabin of his sailing-boat: his rustles then are like those of her undressing husband now.

Ian McEwan is serious, but not solemn, in his unfolding of this predicament, and of surrounding disorders. The painful subject of Edward's 'brain-damaged' mother has its funny side. Marjorie has been struck by a railway-carriage door thrown open by a disappearing toff, and been rendered more or less useless about the house. She fills an eternal scrapbook with cuttings, paints ineffectual watercolours, and is demurely self-deprecating about the meals cooked by her headmaster husband: 'I do hope you enjoy this. It's something new I wanted to try.' The house is a tip. 'The accepted view locally – or this was all they ever heard – was that Mrs Mayhew was artistic, eccentric and charming, probably a genius.' Marjorie's trouble is not obscured or belittled by the comedy it evokes.

The scene where, in their house in the country, Edward's father lets him know, while he is still a boy, what his mother's condition means is very persuasive. It might be felt to be more contingent than thematically-compelled, but it has its place in the story. This is just how someone like that would then and there say something of the kind. Florence's mother is an Oxford philosopher of the modern world, Iris Murdoch's thin and thorny friend, who puts people right and goes to conferences. She too has a place in the story.

The composer of music in McEwan's novel *Amsterdam* (1998) aims to create a pleasure at once 'sensual and abstract, to translate into vibrating air this non-language whose meanings were for ever just beyond reach, suspended tantalisingly at a point where emotion and intellect fused'. The composer's florid creativity is itself beyond reach, uncertain; and in the final pages of the novel it is denied a triumph. And yet the ambition spoken of here is one that may possibly relate to the cultivation of uncertainty apparent in some of the earlier fictions. The present novel is not, in this sense, beyond reach, and the association between outrage and uncertainty, mystery and atrocity, noticeable in his novels and in many novels of the past, is also missing. This helps to portray it as a less romantic work than most of his others.

His earlier fictions show a concern with much else besides outrage. He has written in the past about sexual awakenings and oddities, about second childhoods – reversions to a childish state – and about lost children, and about partners estranged by crisis or bereavement. Old themes are sometimes traceable in the new book, but there is no sense of having been here before. *On Chesil Beach* achieves its overwhelming suspense without recourse to romantic fabulation, to mystery and imagination, or to brilliant tricks and turns. Those readers, however, who see a difference between this book and some of his earlier ones can hardly fail to see that it is richly preceded in these earlier books, and may feel that there is no need to talk of a regeneration, secured by a flight from romance. Such talk belongs to the history of McEwan's engagement with the traditions of Romanticism, an engagement which has come and gone within his work, which has inspired him and which he can't be due to desert. Meanwhile the new book is at least as good as any he has written. It is no pastoral, and it is not a book by a country writer. But it happens in the country – a country of the present time which is never far from its city.

Seamus Heaney shares a Dublin bench with Patrick Kavanagh's effigy.

6

WHAT HAPPENED
TO SEAMUS HEANEY

Seamus Heaney believes in keeping going. He has a poem in which a brother does this, and he has done it himself. He believes that a poet, having started, should start again later, turn a new leaf from time to time, and this he has also done. Steadfast and mutable – *Stepping Stones*[33] accommodates both Seamus Heaneys.

The book is a collection of questions and answers, compiled, largely by correspondence, over a period of some seven years. The compiler Dennis O'Driscoll – poet, senior tax inspector, strict questioner – persuades you that there will be no tolerance of arrears for Heaney here. The replies are tantamount to, while not pre-empting, an autobiography, by someone who says he 'inclines to discretion' but is not a 'self-concealing person'. This is a forthright, though not a confessional book, inclined both to 'elevated stuff' and to jokes. A painter of his portrait

was unfailingly friendly and funny; but even in the mornings, which was when the sittings occurred, he would be hard at the Guinness, and since he had a reputation for being a dangerous drinker, I was constantly watchful. And this is what Edward faithfully painted, the poet vigilant.

He has kept going around the world, but has long been based both in and not far from Dublin, where he has been in the habit of returning in his poems to his early days on the farm in Ulster, and has entered into what can seem like a restored alignment with the religion of the Northern minority. A Catholicism of the imagination is voiced in the book, in contrast with his position in the Sixties, when he would have been 'diffident' in answering questions about the teachings and ceremonies associated with the 'first visionary world' of this cradle Catholic. So his fresh starts have included reversions, and the book is particularly interesting in its discussion of the scope of this born-again imaginative Christianity – if that is not to overstate, for there was never an outright abeyance or denial.

God is no longer dead, at all events, as Heaney may have been moved, with his generation, to wonder in the Sixties. The poet sees ghosts, and his poetry, when it began in him, was experienced as a 'redemptive grace'. There is, if not an afterlife, an 'afterimage of life'. This does not make him the defender of a theocratic Irish Catholic Church, but it may be that he has followed a different course from those of its flocks who are now less faithful than they once were. He would be prepared to admit, I think, that the authority of the Church has been seriously impaired. And yet it can also be said that the course he has followed bears some resemblance to that of the novelist John McGahern, a former victim of ecclesiastical bigotry whose *Memoir* shone with a holy light.

Heaney started in the family farmhouse of Mossbawn in Derry, a steading reminiscent, in certain respects, of the houses lived in by the young Robert Burns. His silent father was a cattle dealer with a bit of land, and both parents are cherished in fine poems of his. He went to school as a boarder in Derry City, then to college in Belfast, then south to a cottage in Wicklow, where he still spends many of his richest hours, then to a Dublin house, with stays at Harvard. He had become a happily married man and the father of three children. He had also become Famous Seamus – a name conferred, he supposes, by Clive James. A huge talent had earned a huge fame. 'A farmer's son from Derry', as he reflects here, had 'ended up behind the lectern' in Oxford's Examination Schools – and at Harvard and in Stockholm. A writer whose sales are thought to amount to four-fifths of those of the poetry published in this part of the world, a man greatly liked by those who know him. There were bound to be complaints.

Stepping Stones pays more attention to these than might have been expected, and it may be that they were more hurtful to him than friends felt at the time. His 'adversary critics' have read the poems 'as statements of a political position', Helen Vendler has observed. It's true that *North*, that momentous new leaf, with its buried bog queen and its sacrificial victims of the past and of the present, was quarrelled with by old friends in the North for reasons that could be termed political: for these critics, he suggests, it was 'an aestheticisation of violence'. But I doubt whether the complaining *literary* criticism which has been received has made much of his leaving the North for the South or refusing to back the terrorist element in the Republican tradition where his loyalty has lain.

He was urged at an early stage to address the Troubles more directly in his verse, in the presumed interest of a new direction for his work: but the truth is that Ulster was present in his poems from the first and that the Troubles – the cruel forty-year civil war which has not always been visible to literary criticism – went on to be a sustained concern. The gun mentioned in one of his first poems, 'Digging', has been interrogated: he now says that the source of the reference was phonetic rather than prophetic, but even if it were absent from the text this would still be a poem about his native place and the condition of Ireland. But it is only very barely a political poem in the sense Helen Vendler intended.

Over in London opposition decried his writing about bulls – the turbines and pylons of the Thirties had taken us beyond bulls. One writer thought him polite and genteel, less savage than Heaney's friend Ted Hughes. His old school friend from Derry, Seamus Deane, called him as 'cautious as a cat', well-in with the powers that be. Hugo Williams called him a good boy. Philip Larkin called him the Gombeen Man, perhaps unaware that the word meant moneylender. Ian Hamilton enquired: 'What *is* a haw-lantern?' He was very good, but minor; he was a parish magazine poet who would never have succeeded if he hadn't been Irish; he was a stage Irishman. It can't have been irrelevant that his British readership at large has always been outstandingly appreciative.

Critics have clearly been vexed by the thought of his good-heartedness. In an interview of 2000 I brashly asked him if he was as nice as he seemed, and he replied that he'd been 'cursed with a fairly decent set of impulses'.[34] A specimen of his candour, and perhaps, of the 'implacable courtesy' which John McGahern, it seems, advised people to deploy in responding to critics.

Some of these objections can be regarded as Britannia's bite-back against Paddy from Derry. Some of them direct one to characteristics discussed in the present book of conversations. It shows, as the poems show and keep showing, how profoundly he is a country writer. Several fascinating pages are devoted to the sheer contents of the house at Mossbawn, with its furniture and scullery and its fetish of a radio aerial let down from a tree to listen to the accents of British broadcasting; and the flit to a nearby place comes across as a paradise lost comparable to the one occasioned by the poet Clare's move to the next village. He lies in bed listening to the horses stirring through the wall and to the adults murmuring through the opposite wall.

The most memorable of his country poems, the expressly rural poems, are often from later life. One of these, 'Two Lorries', has his mother sweet-talked by the coalman, whose lorry is lit by the silken sheen of the sliced coal and its promise of a perfect ash; a second lorry is blown up at the bus station in Magherafelt where he used to meet his mother. The country poems and the family poems display his skills and senses at their utmost. 'My natural bent was to celebrate rather than deconstruct the art of individual poems and poets,' he says in this book. The description of his lumps of coal is another of his celebrations, lodged in a scarcely festive poem.

The interviews look at questions which have been raised over the years as to the dependence of the poems on his personal life and on an autobiographical intent. There is a view – a period view, if you like – that his verse prospers when it can be seen as impersonal, aesthetic, abhorrent of themes and public matters, unparaphrasably private, iconically inaccessible. He ponders the view on this occasion and alludes to Robert Lowell's line 'Yet why not say what happened?' He remarks: 'The dark matter of the news headlines needed to get into *Field Work*, but the light I was hoping for is the kind that derives from clarity of expression, from plainer speaking . . .' This might appear to some to be a cautious no to reportage, or to the claim that his poems should not be seen as governed by an artistic autonomy which departs from what happened. But the claim is worth considering. What happened is palpable and immediate in so much of what he writes best.

Many of his best poems have given and continue to give his response as an artist to the Troubles, that of a generous nature averse to propaganda, apart from a marching song or so on behalf of the peace marchers. The poem in *Station Island* about the murder of a shopkeeper by Protestants, rogue members of the police force who, in order to avoid any air of partisanship, are not identified as such in the poem, illustrates this as well as any. The victim's ghost appears, causing him to apologise for a previous 'indifference' to such deaths. No such indifference can be charged. The horror of the old oppressive 'British' Ulster is treated in the verse, as it is in *Stepping Stones*, with a disciplined coolness. For all its apparition, and for all its discretionary features, the poem tells what happened, while also debating the poet's involvement with the Troubles. His poetry has taught him that 'there's such a thing as truth and it can be told – slant.' Slant or not, and I would think not, the truth is told in this poem.

He has employed, while sometimes distrusting, the power of eloquence, and of the rhetorical. And there are passages of this kind which have been as popular with his native readership as the poem about peeling potatoes with his mother. *The Cure at Troy* is his free translation of Sophocles' play about Philoctetes, cast away on a desert island by the Greek expedition to Troy because of his suppurating wound and despite his unerring magic bow. Odysseus and Neoptolemus arrive, in order to trick him into complying with their demands. The ancient play has been read with recourse to Freudian ideas about the afflicted artist, while Heaney's translation seeks to bring out a contest between individual intransigence and the public good (about to encompass the sack of Troy). He devised a closing choral passage, a public statement of a kind, in which the Ulster peace process can be perceived:

> History says, *Don't hope*
> *On this side of the grave.*
> But then, once in a lifetime
> The longed-for tidal wave
> Of justice can rise up,
> And hope and history rhyme.

It is possible to find a richer poetry in the public-domestic 'Two Lorries' poem, but this passage has its own virtue. Other topical references in Heaney's version of the play he came to regret, but he was grateful to see the lines about hope and history 'enter the language of the peace process', while conscious that 'they belonged in the realm of pious aspiration.' Bill Clinton drew on 'hope and history' for the title

of a book, and 'even Gerry Adams went for the uplift factor.'
Politicians are keen to hold out hope: Barack Obama is the
author of *The Audacity of Hope*, and Clinton was glad to have
been born in a town of that name. They know that much of
this is pious aspiration. But good things do happen, including
the Ulster amelioration, and writers have now and then fore-
told them.

'The famous Philoctetes', as Heaney calls him, is portrayed
in his anguish, by Sophocles, as truthful, kind, unwilling to
hurt. I'd say as a friend that there's a shade of Seamus Heaney
here, of the man whose qualities have been evoked by Dennis
O'Driscoll, who spoke of him recently as a countryman, in
both senses of that word, and praised his 'neighbourliness'.
Wounded or not, this good neighbour has kept going, bow
in hand.

7

YORKSHIRE LAD

The writers of the modern world have said that poetry makes nothing happen, and is no place for the poet's personal life, and that what the reader should care about is not 'the thing said' but the way of saying it. This is a job description which might appear to have gone unheeded by the author of *Birthday Letters*, Ted Hughes.[35]

The thing said in this instance consists of a version of Hughes's seven-year marriage to Sylvia Plath, which ended with their separation and, in 1963, with Plath's suicide. It seems well within the bounds of possibility that this thing, and this way of saying it, will make a difference to the way people feel about poetry, and about marriage, however unlikely it may be that the book will appease the blamers and the defacers who have contributed to the cause célèbre of this marriage by demonising Hughes. We have already heard that Sylvia Plath can't answer back in relation to the self-justifications presumed to be implicit in *Birthday Letters*.

The book is filled with the past and present feelings of its author; we can be sure that he isn't professing or pretending to have them, for art's sake. *Birthday Letters* is, nonetheless, a work of art, and none the less so for being at least as personal and historical as it could be thought mystical or transcendent. The two poets can seem larger than life, their destiny written in the stars. During the seven years of their union, however, their star-crossed feet were often on the ground, as these poems attest.

Oxford's Professor of Poetry (1994–9), James Fenton, is reported to have said that poets have been turning towards the provision of 'information', towards 'content', the thing said; not all of their readers can have noticed this. He suggests that Hughes has been saved from the harm that may attend poetic information by the 'intensity' of what he has written here. Such suggestions take one back to a past involvement of Plath's poetry in the perennial debate about artistic impersonality.

Both Hughes's writings and Plath's are in some measure superstitious, astral. How much magic gets into the weave is hard to assess, for those of mundane outlook who are moved by the poems, while believing them susceptible of a 'domestic' reading – to make use of a term that came into play during this earlier discussion of a transcendent Plath. There's a poem in which she writes that she is 'not mystical'. But then the opposite of such intimations can also appear to be true. The equivocal Plath was both moony and domestic.

The poem here about the couple's recourse to the Ouija board has its intentionally comic moments, as does an earlier prose passage by Ted Hughes on the same subject, where communicative astral bodies are assigned inverted commas – they are 'spirits', these regular attenders at the séances – and one of them is Sylvia's dead father, spoken of at the time as Prince Otto and 'said to be a great power in the underworld'.

In the poem, nevertheless, the Ouija board gives pertinent or at any rate ponderable answers. Hughes is told that 'fame will ruin everything,' while his wife learns that when fame comes,

> You will have paid for it with your happiness,
> Your husband and your life.

Forty-nine is her magic number at one point in the sequence, and Hughes unlocks a certain forty-ninth chamber by means of the skeleton key of a blade of grass.

Domestic readings of Plath's poems were impugned in Judith Kroll's book about her, published in 1976. Its Hughes-approved descriptions tended to remove her work, as far as possible, from the ambit of the confessional or autobiographical. A higher sense was proposed, in which autobiography was subsumed – without, however, disappearing from view – in a mist of dying gods and divine kings. Kroll explained that the marvellous poetry of the end of Plath's days came of a second severance from the divine male. The first severance, Otto's death, which occurred before Hughes knew her, helped to induce a suicide bid, treated by means of electro-convulsive therapy. Kroll also explained that, in 1963, shortly before her death, Sylvia Plath passed beyond the conceptions of mystic rebirth which had mattered to her before, in some eclectic fashion – that she had passed beyond these into a religious transfiguration or conversion. This higher sense has not been forsaken in *Birthday Letters*. But the book can also be called radically domestic.

'Domestic' here does not mean mean or small, doesn't mean knives and forks. The term has to encompass the large and disastrous matter of Plath's father-fixated suffering. These poems abound in responses to those of Plath (they refer to her 'dark water', to her 'peanut-crunchers', lookers-on at the deaths of poets and princes), and have at their heart her exorcistic poem-curse, 'Daddy'. Hughes identifies himself in the book as having been auditioned 'for the male lead in your drama', a drama which is in turn identified as issuing from Otto Plath's premature death. 'Starless and fatherless, a dark water,' wrote Sylvia in *Ariel*. Hughes's book informs us that the loss of her father, and the need to get back to him, and rid of him too, caused, for the pair, the loss of their happiness.

Father-fixation is not named in Nancy Hunter Steiner's memoir of her dealings with her roommate Sylvia at Smith College, *A Closer Look at Ariel* (1974), but can be inferred from it. The memoir corroborates much that is said in these letters to her friend. It persuasively recalls Plath's anxiety, her demands, and finds in her suicide the cry, 'I'll die if you desert me.'

The male victim who can be glimpsed in his letters – to comic effect, at times – is not like the master of his art and of his profession who is apparent elsewhere in Hughes's life and works. But there is no reason to think of this victim as a defensive persona, as tactical or as inauthentic. This is very much Ted Hughes's story, but *Birthday Letters* is not a self-justifying book. It is inhabited by a man who knows that he can be, and has been, mistaken; there is no Lord Hughes of Life, giving out his authorised version.

It is, in this respect, palpably different from the fifty-poem sequence produced by George Meredith a century, to the year, before Plath's death. *Modern Love* is in some other respects almost a precursor; it has a mismating, Meredith's, has demons and the death of a wife, together with the semi-ironic suggestion that poetic content is all right, that 'life, some think, is worthy of the Muse.'

The hundred and more poems in this book are a tale of two cities, Cambridge, England and Cambridge, Massachusetts, with trips to the American wilderness and a last act set in Devon. They come, as do their individual lines, in various shapes and sizes, and are for the most part conversational, indeed epistolary, in manner; they are seldom at all vatic. Each is an episode, an interesting narrative. They have their difficulties, their recalcitrance (a hunter makes his bag of lions 'sound as likely as finished'). But the best of them are among the best poems Ted Hughes has written. Together with his recent *Tales from Ovid*, they are an impressive recruitment and rejuvenation of his powers, those of the supreme country poet of his generation in England.

The Ted Hughes of mid-1950s Cambridge England steps forward here in his black cord jacket, three times dyed. He was seen by companions as a romantic country boy, a Heathcliff, as Lawrentian; lumber-shirted, tall and stalwart, like that other colossus of the time and place, Thom Gunn, a time and place when poets could be 'tough'. There were bystanders for whom he was a gypsy threat to King's Parade and Petty Cury. One don thought that Sylvia could 'pass', as she put it, in any civilised company, but that Sylvia's uncouth, unlettered friend from the country could not. Another don (a good one) felt that Ted's stuff would never do. The future Poet Laureate was at this point the author of 'The Court-Tumbler and Satirist', a poem in the Jacobean style to which he and Gunn were then drawn. 'Princes' are handed there a tendentious view of the artistic life and made to declare:

> Scrambling after girls, bloodying his tusk,
> Groping in the sweat halls for what he can get,
> His fork in any hot dish, the two-backed beast
> Spurring neck and neck with every slut,
> Is how the blood of a true artist makes out.

This true artist was to meet his fate in lipsticked, silver-shod Sylvia, the Veronica Lake 'bang' of hair, as he calls it, shadowing the scar from a scarcely ancient suicide attempt. Here, on the face of it, was a college queen from the conformist American 1950s pictured in her roommate's memoir, from a land of hope and glory where an army of perfect co-ed legs marched towards you in their Bermuda shorts. Beauty and the beast had met. Different backgrounds, different expectations, had met. It must also have been possible to feel that here were two beauties, two stars, two gods, two writers, that a dangerous union was impending.

Towards the start of the book, a letter tells Sylvia that her 'real target'

> Hid behind me. Your Daddy,
> The god with the smoking gun.

Soon he is with her in their Fetter Lane hotel. She is his smooth fish, his 'beautiful America', his new world. But a star warns him to 'stay clear'. The next poem is a formidable articulation of his fate, or part of it:

the grotesque mask of your Mummy-Daddy
Half-quarry, half-hospital, whole
Juggernaut, stuffed with your unwritten poems,
Ground invisibly without a ripple
Towards me . . .

In the poem after this, she is the child who used to rush at visitors, 'clasping their legs and crying: "I love you! I love you!"' – the child who continued to dance for her father. But the poem is concerned with 'the mystery of hatred'. As if 'reporting some felony to the police', the Colleges 'let you know that you were not John Donne.' The colleges of the world would presently bow to her fame, and had already begun to honour her. But it seemed that the return for what she offered was 'envelopes full of carefully broken glass'.

They got married, he says, in the parish church of St George of the Chimney Sweeps: the bride in her pink wool knitted dress, with Hughes 'a post-war, utility son-in-law' wielding a new umbrella, fresh from the bohemian hang-outs of Cambridge England. They are then to be seen in beautiful America, in the academies of New England, and off encountering evil in the deserts of the West. They pay a visit to Yellowstone National Park, where bears have joined the all-American family and gambol at campsites, while able to deliver ninety-mile-an-hour fore-arm smashes. The one that trashes their car is called a ghoul.

Watching Hughes on a seashore through the eye of her camera, she is watching her father, who has risen from the sea. The poet has 'no idea' he has stepped into her sights. She has 'no idea' how a 'two-way heart' and her eye's 'inbuilt double exposure' have brought a double image into focus. A further unknowing concludes the poem.

> I did not feel
> How, as your lenses tightened,
> He slid into me.

In Devon, her eye decrees that New England's beautiful Nauset beach, with its surf and its horseshoe crabs, puts the English coast to shame. The English coast is the extension of a universal English bereavement and subfusc. She is not won over by Woolacombe Sands, which Hughes takes her to inspect, and does not budge from the car.

> A car-park streetlamp made the whole scene hopeless.
> The sea moved near, stunned after the rain,
> Unperforming. Above it
> The blue-black heap of the West collapsed slowly,
> Comfortless as a cold iron stove
> Standing among dead cinders
> In some roofless ruin. You refused to get out.
> You sat behind your mask, inaccessible –
> Staring towards the ocean that had failed you.

Modern poems tend to be no more funny than they are informative. This one is funny. And it could well be the tenderest in the book.

The poem that follows inaugurates the end of the story, with the arrival of a Jewish woman of 'many-blooded beauty' whose fate bears her towards a subversion of the marriage.

She is spoken of as a Lilith – that same Lilith, presumably, who was once a demon and Adam's mutinous, proto-feminist first wife. Presently, the poet is driving down from London along a frozen A30 to fork up his potatoes and gather apples in the garden of their deserted West Country house.

> I picked over my apples,
> My Victorias, my pig's noses,
> In the dark outhouse, and my fat Bramleys.
> My spring prayers still solid,
> My summer intact in spite of everything.

He haunts the house, peering into it as through a keyhole into a casket, the kind of keyhole that might be attempted by a blade of grass. But he 'did not know' that he had already lost the treasure from that casket. Treasures are apt, as here, to be magical, equivocal, ephemeral. In this outstanding poem he is about to discover that the good life is over. Paradise lost.

8

HOT FOR BOSWELL

Such is the fascination, the compulsion, of Boswell's life of Boswell, as recounted in his journals, that there are many of its occasions which any biographer might want to retell – and, at times, in Boswell's own words. One such occasion is the battle of the bugs in Glen Moriston.

Son of an Ayrshire and Edinburgh lawyer-laird with aristocratic connections, Boswell met Samuel Johnson in 1763, and passed into the fellowship of the Turk's Head, where Johnson resembled Falstaff, as Max Beerbohm noticed, and Boswell would not have minded resembling the Prince. They became an item, with Boswell serio-comically demeaned by his Scottishness, which Johnson was unable to leave alone. Ten years later, in 1773, the two of them set off together for Johnson's phobic Scotland, for the Outer Hebrides, which they never reached. But they did well to get anywhere near. Peter Martin speaks in his biography[36] of 'a journey from neoclassic lucidity to the sublime and obscure regions at the edges of the planet'; what would he have said of a trip to Kamchatka or the Niger? The Scottish Highlands were scarcely the heart of darkness, but they were undoubtedly outlandish, and an adventure. For Boswell's friend Belle de Zuylen (alias

Zélide), Scotland itself was 'a little out of the world'. And so it came about that at the end of August the travellers arrived in the obscure region of Glen Moriston, where they spent the night in a turf hut, with manservant Joseph spreading their own sheets on the bed. Boswell's valuable spouse had warned that they might 'catch something'. Boswell and Johnson 'debated whether to get into bed dressed or undressed. Heroically, Boswell shouted at last, "I'll plunge in! I shall have less room for vermin to settle about me when I strip!"'

Martin's book is very much a retelling. What happened to Boswell is presented with continuous reference to the occasions reported in the journal and in the two journal-conscious biographies by the Yale professors Frederick Pottle and Frank Brady, who deal respectively with the earlier and the later Boswell. Both in and out of his quotation marks, Martin here follows the account as it was originally committed to Boswell's journal of the Hebridean tour, which Pottle edited; the text Boswell later published gives 'less harbour for vermin'. The two of them say their prayers and turn in; the Rambler (aetat 64) winds a coloured handkerchief around his head.

Peter Martin's paraphrase has Boswell 'fancying himself "bit by innumerable vermin under my clothes"'. The other two versions – Boswell's two – give 'the clothes'. But none of the three makes it clear what he means by plunging in – whether he slept in his clothes or in his small clothes or in no clothes at all. All three versions make it a fine scene. And Rowlandson did a picture of it, showing a barefoot but shirted Boswell.

Earlier in life, he could be thought by Lord Kames, and by himself, to resemble Tom Jones. At a Northumberland

House assembly in London, where he has begun to show his paces,

> 'You must know, Madam,' he says to one of the ladies, 'I run up and down this town just like a wild colt.' Her reply confirms his new persona: 'Why, Sir, then, don't you stray into my stable, amongst others?'

Martin observes in a footnote: 'Pottle identifies the lady as Lady Mary Coke.' But Pottle both does and doesn't do this. Having in the past identified the woman, Boswell's 'Lady Mirabel', as Lady Mary Coke, he later wrote that it would 'be less than candid' not to add that Lady Mary wasn't really like that. Lady Louisa Stuart's memoir of this woman – who was 'unique' and 'never contradictory', so that 'you always knew in what direction to look for her' – portrays a grand and snobbish paranoid person, who would hardly have leapt to open her stable door to a blabbing and poorly funded young laird on the loose. But then you never know. This was a swinging London.

There is more to the matter than gossip. Pottle called Stuart 'catty', but many of those who know what she wrote might suppose that, had she been male, he might have called her candid. She is among the most accomplished of the 18th century's memorial writers. She was without Boswell's scope and intimacy, his daring informality, the freedom of his self-disclosure, but there are set-pieces by her which are not inferior to his. Her almost total absence from books about Boswell, where she might be thought to deserve a mention for biographical reasons alone, could be taken to point to a restriction of focus in many accounts of Boswell over the years, due in part to their domination by Johnson and by London. The long-lived Stuart, an Anglo-Scot like Boswell, did not figure in the Johnson circle; her Johnson, so far as she had one, was Walter Scott. She was a sharer in the Stuart blood-royal, and as such, in her social eminence, a distant relative of the aspiring Boswell; and she was the daughter of a prime minister, Lord Bute, solicited for advancement reasons by Boswell, and the sister of Lord Mountstuart, also solicited, whose stay in Italy coincided with Boswell's grand tour. Boswell, however, may not have known that she wrote or even, conceivably, that she existed; she herself believed that to be a published writer would have misbecome her rank and gender. Growing up in the palace of Luton Hoo, she seems to have received from male relatives a foretaste of her treatment in books about Boswell.

In Ayrshire, Robert Burns lived a few fields away from the Boswell family house at Auchinleck, but is no more visible than Louisa Stuart in many Boswell books. He was snubbed, apparently, when, already famous, he wrote a letter, enclosing poems and scraping acquaintance. Boswell inscribed on the letter: 'Mr Robert Burns the Poet expressing very high sentiments of me.' A class construction might, but need not, be placed on this rejection slip. His attitude to social inferiors is complex. At times, he can seem queer for victims, the apologist for slavery doubling as a champion of under-dogs and of a particular black slave. At other times, not queer enough, for all his supply of high sentiments. He wrote poems about the death of his first illegitimate child which explained, 'I weep for him whom I have never seen'; the second was 'the finest little girl I ever saw'. Neither survived for long.

Martin's retelling is light on some of Boswell's most interesting female friends and associates. There may be readers who would be glad to exchange a few of his gonorrhoeas for a word or two about Belle de Zuylen's admired novels, or for more about Cornish Mary Broad, who, transported to Botany Bay for stealing a cloak, fled from starvation there by stealing the Governor's rowing-boat and crossing the 3,000 miles of sea to Timor with her husband and seven other convicts and her two small children. She was gaoled when she got to London, but Boswell took her part and she was pardoned.

Then there is Margaret Caroline Rudd from Ulster, enchantress and snake, with whom he had what has been seen as his most fulfilling sexual relationship ('thou hast shown me it rational, pure from evil'). Shortly after she had escaped the scaffold on a forgery charge, he introduced himself to this self-styled descendant of the Stuart kings (Boswell, with reason to claim a similar descent, may just possibly have been her unwitting distant cousin) by dropping the name of a friend, or 'friend', of hers, the Scotsman Robert MacQueen, the future hanging judge Lord Braxfield. Her accomplices, the twin brothers Perreau, had been hanged, holding hands. The Perreaus had betrayed her, and she had betrayed and outwitted the Perreaus, one of them her partner. Boswell's electric and equivocal account of his first fatal interview with Mademoiselle Malfeasans, an alias of hers, is sadly abbreviated here. The forger proved to be a reader; on her shelf sat *Johnsoniana* and Pope's 'Essay on Man'. Mrs Rudd knew a lot about man, and lots of men wished to know Mrs

Rudd. Even Johnson would have liked, he said, to have interviewed her.

On the eve of her trial, she went to buy a rich brocade. The canny man in the shop, fearing for his bill were she not to be acquitted, affected to have no scissors. She handed him a twenty-pound note with the remark: 'There is a pair of scissors.' Boswell wrote an affected period poem about her – 'O Lurginclanbrazil, how sweet is thy sound' – in which a man of feeling calls her a deceiver. But she can still enchant him, and when he thinks back to their time in Armagh, 'All the world's a Lurginclanbrazil to me.'

Martin treats Boswell's boisterous and protesting verse as that of a poetaster, while suggesting at one stage that a poetaster is someone you submit poems to, as Burns did to the Laird of Auchinleck. 'He had no interest in vernacular Scots,' Martin says of Boswell at the outset, but he refers subsequently to 'two ballads in sprightly Scots dialect'. One of these was on the Douglas cause, where Boswell embroiled himself on behalf of Archibald Douglas, a magnate who had come under challenge as an impostor and whose second wife, a relative of Lady Mary Coke's, became the close friend of another relative, Louisa Stuart. Of the challengers in the cause, and of their search through a foreign under-class for evidence of a changeling child, he writes like some broad Scotsman:

> Gang ye your ways to Paris town,
> Blow in the lug o' lown and sorner.

Boswell's adult ear, or lug, was galled by Scots speech, but his best poems are, as you might say, either in Scots or inde-

cent, with the man of feeling off on holiday. His earliest memory
of Edinburgh was of watching the Hessian mercenaries who
were over to quell the Forty-Five rebellion. A Jacobitical poem
notes the absence of small clothes, beneath the kilts of
Highlanders, by which David Hume and other Lowlanders
were diverted:

> I saw you buying breeches for your bums;
> But, with your breeches, you were not so stout
> As the bold Highlanders who went without.

Eighteenth-century Scotland can at times seem a little out
of Martin's world. The issue of patronage in the Church of
Scotland – a landlord's right to appoint ministers to livings –
is pronounced 'not consummately interesting'; it was interesting enough to be one of the country's principal bones of
contention for seventy years after that, and to culminate in
the supremely dramatic Disruption of 1843 – the walk-out of
the Wild, the old-style Presbyterian pure among others, from
the General Assembly of the Kirk. On the same page, Boswell's
pamphlet 'Reflections on the Bankruptcies in Scotland, 1772',
which discusses the failure of the Ayr Bank, Douglas, Heron
and Company, is judged 'more interesting than the title
suggests'. Bankruptcy is never dull, and the Ayr affair was a
reverberating crash.

As the author of a study of the Shakespearean scholar
Edmond Malone, Martin is in a position to deal helpfully, as
he does, with Malone's contribution to Boswell's biographical
labours, without implying that he was responsible for the *Life
of Johnson*. But his book lacks research, and inquiry. It is

difficult to call to mind any matter of fact of which anyone who had wanted in the past to know what Boswell was like, and had decided to do something about it, would be ignorant.

The book's leading attraction is its respectful fondness for Boswell. His biographical method is well explained: his way, for instance, of arranging and occasioning the conversations which were the staple of his journalising, his gift for dramatising his serious talks and comic scenes. The book has none of the philistine disparagement of Boswell's art so long familiar in academies of learning and elsewhere.

'Many of the greatest men that ever lived have written biography,' wrote Macaulay. 'Boswell was one of the smallest men that ever lived, and he has beaten them all.' The goose that lays a golden egg is a largely fabulous bird. Macaulay's indefensible paradox – the littleness of the author of a great work – no doubt lent itself to the modern dissociation of authors from their works, and to the vagaries of those experts willing to reduce Boswell's biography of Johnson to the supposed dimensions of its shallow and immoral author. It would appear, however, that this disparagement has in some quarters been softened by the discovery of the journals, for all their hostages to the ill fortune visited on him by his disparagers. It has now become easier than it once was – though Burke is thought to have found it possible at the time – to believe that, so far from being a vulgarisation of Johnson, as Leavis used to make out, the *Life of Johnson* can be reckoned an aspect of Johnson's distinction, as well as Boswell's.

There he goes in his journal – so awful, so wonderful, so Boswell. Few men so unappealing have ever been so appealing. David Hume spoke of the young Boswell as very agreeable but 'very mad', and he himself spoke of his experience of highs and lows, of good resolutions wrecked by drunken outbreaks and 'aphrodisian spasms', in terms both of disease and of an ancient psychology – that of balance, or equanimity. Flighty and volatile, seasonally depressed, deeply and movingly depressed, he was for ever planning to display the Horatian *animus aequus*, to be stable, *retenu*. The colt let loose in London longed, at the time, to be a *semper idem*: 'to bring myself to that equality of behaviour' which would make it quite hard for people to tell 'whether my spirits are high or low'.

He felt himself 'inconsistent', contradictory. He was one thing after another. You never knew in what direction to look for him. 'Heat always bothered him,' Martin writes, 'the heat of sex, of alcohol, of gambling, of gonorrhoea, of his over-active imagination'; but then we find that he also had a high opinion of warmth, and of the imagination. He was 'a Tory with Whig principles', said a depressive friend, Andrew Erskine, who committed suicide two years before Boswell's death; and another old friend, George Dempster, arrived at this early estimate, a preview of Boswell's divided or compounded state:

> there is a great deal of humility in your vanity, a great deal of tallness in your shortness, and a great deal of whiteness in your black complexion . . . a great deal of poetry in your prose, and a great deal of prose in your poetry . . . a great deal of liveliness in your stupidity, and a great deal of stupidity in your liveliness.

The pathology of his life has proved excellent copy, and it is important to register, as Peter Martin does, that he was in many ways, and for all his weaknesses, a successful man. He felt that his inconsistency made him strange, and his life hard. But his readers must sometimes feel that other lives too are strange and hard, contradictory and changeful, governed and ungovernable, unappealing and appealing, just as other people besides Boswell are apt to blow hot and cold on the subject of heat, and that yet another of the Boswell contradictions can be observed here. The incomparable Boswell is not unique. That is not, of course, to suggest that he was a small man or a representative specimen, or that there could be no grounds for thinking him a manic depressive.

His son James's life was beautiful. James tended and encouraged his father during the delirium of sex and drink and dinners which succeeded the publication of the *Life of Johnson*. The book set half the hacks in London on a sneer, but it was soon, and was to remain, a triumph. The triumph did not lift his spirits; it was as if at some level of his tormented consciousness he would have preferred to shine in Westminster Hall as an English lawyer or as a politician in the House of Commons. His son tried to cheer him up: public men 'have not your happy and convivial hours'. Boswell's life embodied a search for independence, and for a father to depend on, and in his son James, at the very end of it all, he found a father. After Malone's death, James saw to the completion, in 1821, of his Variorum edition of Shakespeare.

9

COCKBURN'S LETTERS

Henry Cockburn has never been what newspapers now routinely call an 'acclaimed' writer. Nor was he exclusively a writer. He was a lawyer too, a politician, a historian, and a pioneer environmentalist. Nevertheless, his writings, which were for the most part published after his death in 1854, and which have never been easy to find, have held the attention of readers from that day to this. A generous and skilful selection of his superb letters has long been hoped for, and that book has at last been published, the editor Alan Bell.[37]

Cockburn was born in 1779. His was a Lowland family of lawyer-lairds, members of Scotland's *noblesse de robe*. The Cockburns were connected – in an era of furious connection – to the first family in North Britain, the almighty Dundases. In 1796, the Younger Pitt's minister Henry Dundas received a kinsman's request, for a sinecure, from Cockburn's father. 'Your namesake Henry in spite of every remonstrance and some degree of severity on my part, persists in being a limb of the Law.' Please let him have the Presentership of Signatures. Henry Cockburn (both he and his namesake were often Harrys) did better than that before long, but he was to bite this hand by turning Whig and resigning his post as Depute to the Lord Advocate.

He remained a limb of the law, and went on to shine as a pleader in court. In the course of the 1820s he assembled the *Memorials of his Time*, which was followed by the two volumes of the *Journal*, where retrospect gave way to the immediacy of a chronicle of 'occurrences as they have arisen'. The *Memorials* is a performative text: it anticipates and enacts the Whig triumph of 1832, when the Reform Act delivered an extension of the franchise and a crisis start was made on the Augean stables of the electoral system. 'The Scotch Millennium seems to me to have arrived,' he exulted in 1829. And two years later, despite concerns about the 'extraordinary rise of popular influence', Ireland, the national debt, poor rates, and the 'decline of our commercial monopoly', he exults again. Here is 'the majesty of public opinion – that true representative on earth of Omnipotence, omnipresent, just, instinctive, resistless, the asylum of all right, the exposer of all wrong – established, not in newspapers and in pamphlets, but on the very seat of government! These are the scenes that we have lived to see, and been allowed to assist in promoting.' As Scotland's Solicitor-General in the Grey administration, he helped to write the Scotch Reform Bill. He then joined the bench of judges in Edinburgh. But Harry Cockburn was never to be lost in the Lord Cockburn of his later incarnation.

In a collection of essays on Cockburn, published in 1979 and edited by himself,[38] Alan Bell commended the letters, saying he might one day edit them. His present Introduction says that Cockburn's special claim to fame lies 'in a posthumous reputation still cherished in his native Edinburgh'. Cherished elsewhere too, of course – by John Sparrow in Oxford and John Clive in Harvard, for instance, neither of them diaspora Scots. There is nothing parochial or provincial, or *petit-maître*, about his appeal. But it is true that he is intensely local and intensely Scottish, a man who went little, and only on duty, to the Wen. He did once make a grand tour of the Continent, and found it remarkably like his native country, with Europe harbouring an Arbroath. Displayed in this selection, in his plenitude, is the homely, pawky patrician cherished in his native city.

Alan Bell is a biographer of Sidney Smith, and his edition of Cockburn's letters rests on an expert knowledge of the Edinburgh of Smith's sojourn there, and of the inner circle, to which Cockburn belonged, of the *Edinburgh Review*. Bell's notes are pledged both to locality and to the dates and distinctions of the legal and landed aristocracies of the North. Cockburn was a self-seen 'son of the gentry' who took the liberal side in political contention. He came to the seigneurial view that Walter Scott was not cosy in his Abbotsford nest – what with the disagreeableness of Lady Scott, and his eventual restriction to the company of printers, players and 'low Torries'. His judge's circuit journeys took him round and round his native land like some august gypsy, and his book on the subject abounds in encounters with old laird friends, couthy provosts, the 'worthy' of this place and that, and in a minute attention to the Scotland whose landscapes he loved and whose scowling weathers he deplored. He was a great walker, but Ben This and Ben That were apt to be rained off. Meanwhile poor people are thin on the ground. Of the bathers of Rothesay, some of them nude, he classifyingly observed: 'men and women, ladies and gentlemen, proceed with their respective visits to the sea.'

Whig politics, and the politics of the Kirk, which suffered the Disruption of 1843 when its evangelical, 'Wild' wing walked out of the General Assembly of the Church, 'the Venerable', as it was known, are less prominent here than the human being who engages in these activities but in many others besides. Cockburn, the Lord of Session, admired the mutineer ministers of the Disruption, if somewhat equivocally, for affronting the law of the land and for their possession of an ancient Presbyterian zeal.

Cockburn is thought classical, but was drawn to romantic tastes and initiatives, to a recoil from the 'mathematical' New Town that was going up around him, to ruins, towers, castles. He disliked the 'brilliancy' of Macaulay's prose (his conversation, though, was that of a Flanders draught horse, compared with the 'light fiery Arabianism' of Scotland's brilliant Francis Jeffrey, editor of the *Edinburgh Review*). But he also felt that Gibbon was stylistically unsound, a danger to the young; this might suggest an attraction to the new prose of Dickens and Carlyle, but he can't be said to have written accordingly. He launched into letter-writing in the full flush of a juvenile sensibility. A restless and ambitious young man of feeling, he was hardly in a position to smile at a female correspondent of later years with the injunction that she might at least sit down and write him a letter 'describing your emotions'. His own youthful emotions were described. As time goes by, a wiser and funnier man appears in the letters.

The letters of his maturity, though, remain youthful in so often seeming playful, allusive, figurative, teasing, shocking, and they are sufficiently these things to be a problem at times for any annotator who means, as in this case, to be terse.

There are a couple of interesting times here when more may or must have been known and might have been noted. The poet Thomas Campbell, one of the circle of Cockburn's early friends, produced a couplet about a premarital Adam, lonely in the Garden of Eden:

> The world was sad! The garden was a wild!
> And man, the hermit, sighed – till woman smiled.

When Campbell married, late in life, the news was transmitted by Cockburn: '"Tam the hermit sighed, till woman smiled." Her name is Sinclair – from Liverpool – know nothing about her. No money. This step I take to be more poetical than prudent.' Pegasus would be burdened with such a wife. Meanwhile the Tam joke might have been mediated.

Likewise, a reference to 'an old good natured stammering schoolfellow of ours, Pat. Sellar' carries a note which explains that this was probably a factor of the Earl of Sutherland, but leaves it to be inferred that he was also a prominent enforcer of the Highland Clearances, supposed to have uttered the invidious cry: 'Damn her, the old witch; she has lived too long. Let her burn!'[39] With Cockburn among the counsel for the defence, he was charged with homicide as a result of his activities, and acquitted by a jury of the affluent. Later, as a circuit judge, Cockburn tried a case where tenants had 'rioted' over their eviction. They could not be aquitted, he remarked at Inverness, the majesty of the law had to be upheld. *Fiat lex.* But the conviction 'was founded on most scandalous facts. The people who had sown, and were entitled to reap, their corn, had their houses pulled down, with *no other houses to go to, no poor house, no ship*, nothing but the bare beach to ly upon.' The jury recommended leniency and the sentence was light.

Allusion reaches its apogee in a letter of 1808, where Cockburn denies authorship of a poem, 'Geraldine'. The joke has taken, he told the poet James Grahame.

> You have been censuring one of Shakespeare's best little pieces, modernised by Warton. This is the poem of which Shakespeare says in a letter to a cousin of Spencer's, a relation of Sir Henry Wotton's, 'Well beloved Sire – I send you one of my best litt. pieces ycleped The Holy Grove or Geraldine, composed upon the sadde going awaye of yr nieece . . . So you may criticise Geraldine as you please or dare, being Dick's own.

Who is this Dick Shakespeare? Having attributed the poem to Cockburn in a book published in 1975, *Cockburn's Millennium*, I have since reached the conclusion that it is both by Cockburn and by his great friend John Richardson, who left his romantic town to become a London solicitor, and who married Betsey, niece of the Miss Hills of Woodhall near the Pentland Hills. Cockburn and his friends used to forgather at Woodhall, to go for walks and revise each other's poems, a *cénacle* of Whig romantics.

All this matters more than the poem might seem to be worth. Geraldine was a heroine name of the period (dropped by Coleridge and in Scott's *Lay of the Last Minstrel*), and the poem in her praise forms part of a vast cento of favourite bits of verse – another period feature, an extension of sensibility's commonplace book – patched together by these Whig romantics. The Pentlands anthology, compiled between 1807 and 1809, excludes Shakespeare and includes stanzas of their own, and the choices closely correspond to those of the *Oxford Book of 18th-Century Verse* of 1926, edited by David Nicol Smith, who was keen to show an organic growth of Romantic from pre-Romantic nature poetry; the shock of the new thereby both diminished and enhanced. The anthology, by friends of the recently launched *Edinburgh Review*, which has long been considered hostile to Romantic writers, leads off with two passages, in Cockburn's hand, from 'Tintern Abbey'. He and his anthology set store by the treasuring of favourite places and early scenes. Wordsworth's poem suggests an aspect of Cockburn's complex nostalgia.

He was to rebuild and inhabit an old house nearby, causing it to grow a tower, 'cheered morning and evening by the ring of masons' chisels – those larks and nightingales of architecture. Yet in the surgency of one's own walls there is great delight.' Much of his life was passed at Bonaly, in flight from the law and the city, in pursuit of 'nature and romance'.

The letters are not all larks and nightingales, roses and dahlias and trees. Justice is done to bottoms and bowels. An 18th-century outspokenness gave rise to passages of a kind that was docked from his annals by the Victorian relatives who saw them through the press, and is absent from the marmoreal life, published by him in 1852, of his other greatest friend, Francis Jeffrey: 'no owl more wise, no lark more aerial'. A Rabelaisian passage, as if translated by Sir Thomas Urquhart, admonishes his admired Lord Advocate friend Andrew Rutherfurd:

For God's sake, Andrew, take care of your eyes. Severe Students too are very apt to suffer sorely from their bowels . . . Do call at Alexander the druggist's shop in Dundee and ask for the Idler's pill, or the Scholar's belly salve, or the Sedentary man's doup plaster, or the Student's windy cordial, or the Philosopher's clearer, or the Lawyer's delightful pocket companion, or the Judge's rectifier, or Vacance Powder – or anything else that will keep you as well and make you walk as stately as during the idleness of last winter.

This advice to 'Aundra' (Scots for Andrew) follows on the tale of a stately fall from a horse before the very eyes of Edinburgh:

Richardson made the most beautiful descent yesterday in Maitland Street from the back of a tall grey hack you ever beheld. It was a stupid brute, totally incapable of making one unnecessary motion, and it lay so slowly and patiently down upon its knees and its nose, while the sollicitor pitched so effectually upon his best London hat, and then rolled so thoroughly over upon his clean brushed *Town* greatcoat; danger being quite out of the question, from the pacific indifference with which the beast stood still and snorted the dust off his mouth, and the unintended neatness with which John's feet came out of the stirrups – as if for the very purpose of not impeding him in his plunge; while there were just enough of spectators to enjoy it and give it a zest, and not so many as to make it shameful; and then the half jocose ruefulness with which he led the dirty kneed steed back to the stable, with an unconscious dimple in the said hat, his discomfiture marked

on his dirty back, his cane bent useless, everybody smiling
(and he seeing this) at the impossibility of either getting quit
of the beast, or of mounting him again; the day's ride visibly
quite spoiled, tho' the hire must be paid, and the chairmen
galling the wounded spirit by running from sundry quarters
offering him their aid.

In 1832, an MP in London is advised to 'attend to his viscera'
(while, in Edinburgh, the cholera is about to arrive at the
Water of Leith). On another occasion, a judge has been 'operated in the Rectum'. In his final year, he himself has been
'under what old Miss Auchterlonie always called Bumlago'.
His contribution to the nether language which was at one
time unpublishable should not be ignored; it was that of an
expert on the cleansings and clearings of an age which witnessed
a need for order and invention, in which hygiene made strides
but still had a lot to step over. One of his rears, published in
the essay collection of 1979, is omitted here. In 1831, at the
centre of the city, a public lavatory, or 'cloaca maxima', as he
calls such places elsewhere, was rooted out to make room for
the Royal Institution building which preceded the Royal
Scottish Academy.

On the 1st of March – being the day on which the motion
for Reform was made in Parliament, the bog began to be
moved at the Institution. In both it is a clean sweep. But I
must confess that walking out yesterday to the Foul Brig I
saw the sun glittering three times on a large, distant, whitish
object, which, being neared, turned out to be a bum.

He was a defender of Edinburgh's artists, and of its beauties and ancient monuments. For all his protests, however, a railway was driven through the heart of 'the Shitty of Edinburgh', whose ancient stinks had yet to be reformed.

'Any soft-minded person would have pitied them,' said a crofter of his own evicted generation. Cockburn was a compassionate man, but far from soft. On poor relief, he was no enthusiast for the assessment of landowners for that purpose; he favoured self-help, and thought that paupers and criminals should not be made better-off than the honest poor. And here he is on legs:

no doubt, generally speaking, two are better than one; chiefly because after one is gone, there is only one more to go. But I can never forget the case of a nice, merry, warm hearted, Hebe looking, English girl, who thirty years ago was the greatest friend of Mrs Cockburn and her sisters and associates, and is still an attached, Scotch-living intimate. She came to me in great agitation, to consult about an offer she had just got, of marriage. She had hardly any relations, and not a penny; nothing but her beauty, her sunny gaiety, and her excellent virtues. The offerer was one of the best living men, very rich, universally popular, good looking, and very agreeable – but minus a leg. It was an offer worthy of the first girl in the land, and seemed to me like a special Providence to her. But, like an ass, she would not swallow the leg – in spite of all my demonstrations that the want of it, by making him more domestic [than] otherwise, was a positive advantage. It stuck in her throat. Some years after, she captivated a biped – a laird and a soldier; and another lady, a friend of her own, gave her heart to the surviving leg. What was the result? They are both now widows, each having lost her only child. But the spouse of the uniped lived respected and happy, and beloved by her husband, and is now mistress of a large jointure and a gorgeous house. She of the biped got two legs, and a drunkard . . .

It may not be possible to imagine that Jane Austen might have wanted to write this story, and it is doubtful whether Mrs Cockburn would have wanted to hear it from her husband.

She was a large, perhaps winsome woman with spreading skirts and a maternal lap. He ascribed to her the remark, made when he became a judge: 'Odd – Preserve me this! I never slept wi' a Lord o' Session i' my life!' This, though, is not the woman who, rarely glimpsed in the letters, is shown there on other occasions as fussy and nervous. On circuit with him four years later, in 1841:

my lady really did all she could to be happy and easy. But she is sadly oppressed by the terror of impropriety, and is a visible check on any tendency towards indecorum, or even levity, on the part of her learned Lord. But, if it be often enough repeated, I would not wonder if our vulgar mirth, and hand shaking baillies, and dunches [biffs] from waiters, and travellers looking into her bed room when it won't lock, and retiring with an apology, and the upsetting of tea kettles ill balanced on the fender, etc., should soften her into some practicable pliancy.

Cockburn is joking here, but the joke does not prevent this from looking like a revealing glimpse. His letters are filled with jolly and contented cries, with a relish of fine days, birds and flowers, the claret and coal fires of a redoubtable conviviality; they are not expansive about the recesses of his domestic life; the pain that can be read in the portraits of him is seldom expressed. There are exasperations about sons whom he blames for the financial difficulties which overtook him, and which he overcame. But if these are not confessional letters, his privacy is guarded there less resolutely than it is in his memorial writings, and the dispatching of letters to his men and women friends was clearly liberating to him. Alan Bell's edition communicates a more intimate Cockburn than has been visible to most of his readers, and the truth is that impropriety, indecorum, could prove an inspiration.

Priests were mad, he would say; certainly roaracious and bletheracious. But there were members of the Venerable (Thomas Chalmers, Sir Harry Moncreiff) whom he venerated. One minister suspected him, when he was young, of having deserted 'even my religious *profession*'. This was a false alarm. Cockburn's was, in his own expression, 'a rational piety', closer to nature than to the fissile Kirk.

He was commemoratively close to his gardening mother, remote from his father, a queller of riots, a mere agriculturalist on his Granton estate, with his domestic 'degree of severity'. Cockburn was himself pugnacious. To resort to anachronisms, he was both right and left, neither Jacobite nor Jacobin, and it seems fitting that his descendants should include both Evelyn Waugh ('I would like to be descended from a useless Lord') and the buccaneering left-wing journalist Claud Cockburn.

His reason was with the modern world, he said, his dreams with the past. He was a patriotic Scotsman who wanted Scotland brought 'within the action' of the British constitution: a threat, of a kind, to his class and country, to the old Scotland he wished both to keep and to clear away.

Let there still, he felt, be ladies and gentlemen. 'Reform that you may preserve,' in the words of Macaulay, or in those of Lampedusa's *Leopard*, concerning the Sicilian nobility: 'If we want things to stay as they are, things will have to change.' Cockburn's electorate of North British males was only modestly enlarged and improved in the year of jubilee, and there were hard times in store for Scottish poverty. Popular influence, nevertheless, was on the march, and there can be no doubt that he did want to change certain things. He wanted free speech, a wider politics, a check to the hereditary system.

In 1828, in one of the reformer's less buoyant moods, he confessed that he expected 'no good thro' public men now, or likely to be, in power; and my only hope is in the steadiness and improving character, and encreasing force, of public opinion'. As for the King, 'I have long had a desire to be King myself. I am quite satisfied that I would be the best monarch Britain ever had; which shows how ill it has been served.' It is his grasp of what it might mean to talk of the majesty of public opinion which makes him a statesman of consequence. The meaning he embraced was at once restrictive and greatly enabling. In his book on the Sedition Trials of the 1790s he wrote:

In those days there was no tolerance for the assumption of any opinion by the lower orders. The very term *the people* was used sparingly, and always with aversion. The *public* was the word for the middle ranks, and all below this was the *populace*, or the *mob*.

The semantics of Cockburn's triumphal Whiggism hovered between the claim that the people had arisen and the more persuasive claim that the public had arisen, in the sense that the middle ranks had spoken. While continuing to fly the Whig flag of sense and justice, he feared, as he grew old, a further extension of the franchise, the doom of a universal democracy. It would be in Russia first, he thought. Lawyers and historians would not in years to come be slow to blame him – for indolence, arrogance, for drafting errors made as Solicitor-General, some of which preserved abuses and permitted a fresh manufacture of votes. He was aware that such errors had been made. To Andrew Rutherfurd's wife Sophia he wrote in 1839 of a need 'to cure the since discovered defects which defeat the Reform Bill'. But he was entitled to pride himself on having sped 'the progress of some of the greatest measures that ever engaged the reason or the passions of parliament or of the public'.

He was among the most beneficent of Scotland's, and England's, political thinkers, and one of the best of their narrative historians. He was as combative and as principled as another Edinburgh politician, Robin Cook – each of them a hill walker, neither of them tall, sneered at for that by the discerning media. All honour to these bonny wee bristling birds.

10

MCNEILLIE'S DREAM

John McNeillie was an Anglo-Scottish writer who made his reputation as a novelist of country life and as its journalistic chronicler. His work belongs to the rich vein of rural literature, much of it retrospective, some of it consolatory, which came to publication over the years that ran from the Depression to the aftermath of the Second World War. He was to publish under two names: his own and the pen name of Ian Niall, who was the author both of novels and of rural pieces in *Country Life* and the *Spectator*. Two of his best-known novels, *Wigtown Ploughman* (1939), his first, and *No Resting Place* (1948), are by John McNeillie and Ian Niall respectively. Born in 1916, he lived successively in Scotland, England and Wales. He is – to use a term of recent provenance – a distinctly archipelagian writer.

He spent several years on a Galloway farm, under the wing of his paternal grandfather, formerly a blacksmith. There were to be two expulsions from Eden – a first separation from his parents in Glasgow was compounded by a departure from the farm at North Clutag.

Whenever I am under stress I retreat into that world I knew

as a child. I see the morning sun coming up behind the Galloway hills. I smell the salt ham frying. I chase bees and trap them in a bottle half full of clover heads and I get drunk on the smell of peat reek, old tea roses and honeysuckle. I suppose I was never fit for the real world.[40]

The literary critics of his lifetime were given to a censure of nostalgia, with its beguiling talk of a vanished countryside and its alleged unfitness for a 'real world'. McNeillie's nostalgia, however, while dream-like at times, is a complex country matter, and his writings are often far from consolatory. He has been seen as a realist. He has also been seen as wild and reclusive. For all his fluency, there was a certain silence in him.

A Galloway Childhood, published in 1967 and assigned to Ian Niall, is an excellent book, a vindication of nostalgia. His grandfather figures as an Old Testament patriarch whose prophecies come true. On a visit to London he foresaw that the Thames would overflow its banks, which it did the following year, swamping Chelsea. He was also a patented inventor, who made a steel arm for an amputee which was wielded more than successfully in a mêlée. 'Haste ye,' said the household, where a celestial slavery obtained. In an earlier version of the memoir, *My Childhood*, recovered from an attic and assigned in 2004 to John McNeillie, 'it was always time for something or other.' The memoirs nevertheless suggest that, as Flora Thompson said in 1939, in *Lark Rise to Candleford*, of the country folk of her remembered past, they were happier than those who came after them.[41]

The boy was enclosed at North Clutag in a stupendous kinship, entranced, while sometimes craving to be up and away, to be 'the wild creature I really was'. His women set themselves to civilise him. He was made to know his place, but was also cherished; as were horses and ponies, which were tantamount to people – seen and not heard, but you could talk to them. John McNeillie came to think more highly of certain animals than of the run of human beings.

Harvests were at the centre of things. 'Unless you have lived to watch the corn grow and ripen, and have known that peculiar excitement that comes to a climax in autumn, it may be hard to understand what harvest meant in the days before the combine and the baler.' McNeillie was proud to have been farmed out, and proud of his forebears, while persuaded that others felt compromised by such origins.[42]

After North Clutagh came a move with his immediate family to Ealing, where he was known, at school, as an intimidating foreigner. He worked as a reporter on the *West Middlesex Gazette*, and slipped down the back of a woman's dress at a dance – the woman he was soon to marry – a teasing note: 'John McNeillie. One day this name will be famous.' They settled in Colwyn Bay, where a contribution to the war effort brought him the management of an engineering factory. Meanwhile he explored a wild Wales, where he spent a good deal of his remaining years shooting and fishing. A second 'moonlighting', that of a busy writer, was also in operation. There were books based on or akin to his rural pieces in the London journals, among them *The Poacher's Handbook* (1950) and *A Galloway Shepherd* (1970). In 1949, he brought out the novel *Foxhollow*, a barbed comedy of missing persons and neighbourhood spies, some scenes of which have the sombre, sinister strength of Sickert's domestic interiors. A few months before that, he wrote his favourite novel, 'The Wick Burned Low', which was never published.

In his first novel poaching is rife, and the book is full of fights, as is *No Resting Place*. The Wigtown ploughman, Andy Walker, is a terror and a bonny fechter. The whacks are soberly recounted: they have the same degree of structural importance as, but are without the operatic extravagance of, those enacted in the American television series *The Sopranos*. In both cases, the humanly sympathetic can lend themselves to the whacking. Andy is shown as a stubborn, hostile man set down in a Hiberno-Scotland, an Irish Galloway. These two novels contrast with the paradisal memoirs and with the less adversarial later writings in general. Both eirenic and embattled, his writings present a divided Galloway, a Galloway of war and peace. The two novels are dark and severe about what goes on in the hinterland, and the first of them fed at once into a concern and outcry for the improvement of agricultural living conditions. Attitudes to sex and drink are spoken of as brutal. Illegitimate children are as common on the page as lawful ones. Women are now and then 'sluts'. And yet there's a feeling which few readers could doubt for the men and women who lead these lives.

The young Andy is admitted to the world of blows when his father, also an Andy, finds him, on returning from work, shut out of the cot. Inside, the Andies discover a scene of clandestine love – a country-customary transgression, as it has long been perceived. Wee Andy's father plunges into a series of assaults on his wife Sarah and her companion, who heads off. Sarah is shut out, but creeps back in when her husband hastens to the pub in his topcoat to boast of his achievements.

'She sat down by the fire and sobbed as she tenderly felt her lacerated face.'[43]

Wee Andy grows up to re-enact such scenes and to marry a wife who has been exposed to incestuous abuse, and has the guts to stand up to her husband as the novel moves to its close, with Andy excelling in the ring at a fairground but choosing not to turn professional. The country reclaims him. He was 'not like other men': but there were others in the region whose fists flew and whose fates were much the same.

Alec Kyle, leading man of *No Resting Place*, which was made into a film by Paul Rotha, is one of a band of tinkers in an indeterminate Galloway or Ireland. They are up against the Poliss, and their women and children aim 'insults of amazing vulgarity' at the farmers they fall out with. On their way to thin a farmer's turnips they are challenged by a keeper, and in the course of the opening twenty pages various bodily harms are recorded: an effect of burlesque is approached, but never reached. These harms include the keeper's manslaughter by Alec Kyle of the withered arm, which is followed by a punishment beating of Alec by a brother. On the road that day, Alec's wife Meg 'wished she had never seen him; wished he and she had never been born'. By the end of the novel, however, the bond between them, and Alec's love for his children, have been made clear.

The local town is a community where only the scum are said by the writer to speak to its nomads, to the displaced, the illegal, though he also indicates that farmers and their wives speak to them in the line of business, and can even be friendly with them. McNeillie is attached in these two novels to wandering and rebellious people, while also conceding to the voice of the settlements which complains about disorder and vulgarity.

McNeillie's storytelling is admirable, and ancestral. His kin were keen on stories, and he could lay claim, as could James Hogg, to a storied witch among his forebears. His feeling for landscape is equal to that of John Buchan (whose ear for the voice of the settlements was rather more acute). The harshness to be met with in his fiction recalls the Ayrshire writer George Douglas Brown's *The House with the Green Shutters* of forty years before. Lewis Grassic Gibbon's series of novels, *A Scots Quair*, which drew to an end when McNeillie began to publish, is likely to have influenced him, though the comparison with McNeillie's writings, in their copious leanness, has been felt by some to reveal in his predecessor a romantic country life and a recourse to the poetic. His attention was captured, when he set out to write, by the American realists of the mid-20th century, chiefly John Steinbeck; his principal affinities may have lain with Hemingway and with D.H. Lawrence. But he was a writer who wanted to light out in his own way for the wild.

His interest in aggression was in large part mandated by the environments he chose to write about, and was expressed at a time of war and impending war when fiction had come round to a new candour in the portrayal of sex and violence. It was also markedly ambivalent. He fought his corner in the playground and went on to a 'slaughter' of the 'poor creatures of the wild' ('one clean blow and he is dead').[44] But, for all his domestic short temper, he was against the use of corporal punishment on his children – unlike his father, apparently – and his communion with animal life is among the most appealing attributes of his work.

Tam o' Shanter would not look out of place in McNeillie's Galloway, a region of Burns's South-West of Scotland, and Burns's poem about him is known to McNeillie's characters, men who can't read. After beating up his wife and her lover, Andy's father lands up in the pub, and then, on his way home, he

> stopped and relieved himself in the middle of the road, and began to recite a passage of Burns's most popular work. He ranted on, reeling off the adventures of 'Tam o' Shanter'. The words were hopelessly muddled. He kept trying to remember them, but his throbbing head refused to recall the exact version. A woman on a bike came towards him. The light of the carbide lamp almost blinded him. She was a servant girl from a farm not far away.
>
> 'Comere,' he mumbled and staggered over as if to catch at her.[45]

'Catch at her' echoes the language of Burns's poem ('The carlin claught her by the rump'), which may indeed have lent a little to this episode. McNeillie's stories convey that a keener appetite for the depiction of violence had arisen in the literature of Western societies. Neither the adolescent Burns nor the adult Hogg could stomach Shakespeare's *Titus Andronicus*, as it happens. But it would be wrong to take it that the Scottish countryside was then a milder world. Both the Ayrshire ploughman and the Border shepherd were on occasion compelled, as John McNeillie was, by the imagination of physical harm.

11

GLASS'S LIFE OF GRAY

'"Be my Boswell!" he shouted, dancing a jig around the room and raising a finger to the heavens. "Tell the world of my genius!"' This is the Scottish writer and artist Alasdair Gray, frisking with the author of his biography.[46] James Boswell was sneered at for being Johnson's spaniel. Rodge Glass, a Jewish Mancunian who went north to study Creative Writing with Gray, and who then served as, while eventually for some reason ceasing to be, his secretary, can come across at times as a rather larger creature, bounding along and 'bouncing' about, as he says himself, in tune with his master's achievements, helping with his plights and postponements. His book is friendly. It is also frank.

At one point he meets up with his master in mid-afternoon Edinburgh. Gray is due to address one of his many meetings in the evening, and has been drinking. They set off down the steep Royal Mile, and end up in a Siamese tangle at the foot of it, as if to celebrate the devolved Scotland then, perhaps, in parliamentary session nearby: Gray, a do-what-you-want democrat, has always wanted a separate, republican Scotland, and may have his doubts about devolution, but must surely be quite pleased with the arrival of government at Holyrood.

After the tumble he made it to the meeting, let it be said. Few biographers can ever have come so close to their subject.

Glass has no desire to behave as a patient scholar or as a discursive critic. His footnotes are of the kind that tells you well-known writers are well-known, and one of them appears to know very little about Edmund Wilson. His book is almost as much about what it was like to write it as it is an anatomy of Gray's life and work. 'Not only do I care greatly for Alasdair, but I also wish him to care greatly for me.'

This promotes an intimacy and contributes to what is, in its way, a successful book. Gray is made vivid, as is his member- ship of the remarkable generation of West Coast Scottish writers which got going after the Second World War – Archie Hind, James Kelman, Agnes Owens, Tom Leonard, his lifelong friends. The early life, and the early recruitment of his powers, are of great interest: the fireside dramas, the bed-settee, the school magazine, the public library, the Butler Education Act, which, as Gray acknowledges, did much for working-class children – such mentions are likely to bring pangs of recognition to anyone who was there or thereabouts at the time. We are in that unforgotten country where pleasure came before a fall, where you were advised to enjoy yourself when you could, while you were still young.

Glass's candour ranges widely. Is Gray's art – his drawings – important? *'What if it has been ignored because it's no good?'* Gray is shown peeing into the sink in mid-dictation. A close woman friend is cited: 'He's the nicest man I've ever met – I just couldn't take the drinking.' His 'head-shaking' second wife, Morag, seems at one stage to be 'acting as a counter- balance to the cuddly treatment he gets from everyone else'.

The circumstances of his birth suited the legend, the hero, that he later became in Scotland, and beyond, when his fiction was reviewed and read in London and 'even', as Glass puts is, in Los Angeles. His granny refused to let her daughter into the house when her waters broke, and his father had to cycle round Glasgow for medical assistance. Panic, Gray has suggested, with reference to this refusal. His parents were good to him, apparently, with his mother somewhat occluded in Glass's record and in his own autobiographical accounts; and he has a sister of independent mind. He grew up in the Riddrie district of the city, was the 'dreamy' one that used to be detected in Scottish schools of the period, went to Glasgow Art School, and became a reluctant teacher. He had begun, and was to continue, to suffer from eczema and from asthma. Success, when it arrived, could be arduous too. 'I thought to myself – *I am now a famous and established man! I must now be able to make some kind of living* . . . I soon realised this was going to be more difficult than expected, and I thought, *Oh fuck!*' This expletive is over-used now in print: here, it is exquisite.

The legend of Alasdair Gray was to embody that of Gulley Jimson, hero of Joyce Cary's novel of the period, *The Horse's Mouth*. It has also embodied a version of the Faust story, in which he has taken an interest. Gray can come across as a Dr Faustus whose potions and alembics would sometimes miscarry but who, as with his Canongate tumble, has kept going.

He married Inge Sorensen, a Danish nurse, by whom he had a son, but the marriage rapidly went wrong, and this would seem to have led to a chronic preoccupation with sexual difficulty. His life can appear to be enclosed in the dream of rejection which ensued. 'Being bad at sex' was 'one of his favourite subjects'. In the late Eighties Inge returned dying to the flat where he lived with his new wife Morag, asked to be taken in, and lay for a while in the marital bed, before moving elsewhere for her last few months. 'It is hard to believe that he could not have just gently refused her request,' writes Glass. There is a great deal of Gray in this refusal to refuse.

In 1981 he published his most famous book, *Lanark*, which had undergone a gestation of many years.[47] The novel, or more than novel, folds together two stories, that of the man Lanark and that of Duncan Thaw. The two men are held together by the magnetism of duality; they are the same but different. According to Glass, 'Thaw *thinks* life instead of living it, and Lanark *does* life without thinking it.' They are united by a surliness, a refusal to please, which marks them off from most other suffering sensitives in the literature of the modern world. They speak as they find. The Lanark material which surrounds the Thaw narrative is expressed in fantastic terms, and also, though the link has been disowned, in Science Fiction terms. The Thaw narrative is virtually naturalistic and is a novel in its own right, largely based on features of the Gray agon. To say that it is humanly superior to the rest of the novel – outcome of those long years of contemplation and elaboration – is to risk indictment as an enemy of the ludic and the fantastic, of magic realism, of the post-modern. Speaking as I find, I think it is a risk worth taking. What chiefly matters is that the Thaw narrative is a wonderful evocation of the dark, interesting Glasgow of Gray's youth – of its weathers and waters and overcast skies, its outspoken folk, with their pursuit of art and knowledge under all this inclemency. Glasgow may be more of a Capital of Culture than Edinburgh will ever discover.

'Nothing less than an epic, I decided, was worth writing,' reports the Tailpiece in *Lanark*. Gray has taken a relaxed view of what an epic is, and he shares it with James Hogg, who claimed in one of his hyperboles that his satirical verse saga, *Queen Hynde*, was Scotland's 'best epic poem'. This view of epic is among the affinities which bind together these two versatile writers. It is also a reason for the elaborations that encircle the Thaw narrative.

Both the Glass narrative and Gray's fictions raise questions relating to fame and neglect, and the fate that awaits the lover of women. The impression is given that he became popular when he became famous. Women threw themselves at him then, one woman said. Late in *Lanark*, Lanark is at his curtest when told by one of these women of Gray's: 'Bet you enjoy being famous.' 'I'm not,' replies Lanark. 'Modest, eh?' 'No, but I'm not famous either.' A few pages later, Lanark is 'suddenly a famous man with important papers in his briefcase. Women loved him.' Meanwhile the woman who thought Gray was the nicest man she'd ever met said that there were times when it could seem that he 'just wasn't thinking of anyone else' but himself. They are still friends. The problems Gray faced in this quarter enter profoundly into his writings. They are not the stuff of gossip. In discussing the biographical implications of a rape fantasy projected in Gray's work, Glass remarks: 'we do not usually make that connection between author and art, so why make it here?' Elsewhere in his book, biographical connections are made to considerable effect, but it's certainly true that such connections can give rise to puzzles. Will Self was to cut the present knot with the claim that with Alasdair 'the maker and the made are 100 per cent the same thing.'

In *1982, Janine*, published shortly after *Lanark*, fantasy is present in high concentration. Rapes are imagined. Political discourse co-exists with satirico-sado-masochistic reveries. Suspense is missing. Characters are phantasmal. Ten years later came what is widely seen as one of his best books, *Poor Things*, a Stevensonian-Shavian tall tale of medical men of Faustian predilection in Victorian Glasgow: Bella Baxter is a *belle dame sans merci* who teaches the lessons of a humanitarian socialism. It has the rival narratives of Hogg's *Confessions*. Witty and ingenious and well-told, it bears witness to what the fantastic has been able to do for Gray.

In 2007 he was heard to complain that in the field of modern art 'he and his contemporaries had been ignored.' He could hardly have said the same about his own literary reputation. Having survived the *per ardua ad astra* of the mid-century ambitious Scot, he has been famous for a long time now: troubled, cuddled, with the scars to show for his celebrity – *per astra ad ardua*. As caught in Glass's mirror, a charming, irascible man in the Scottish mould. Charm is not supposed to be popular in his native city, but an exception has been made for Gray. He has not been locked out of the world of publicity: he has had his agent, his secretary, his various London publishers and his fan following, and this book comes to an end in what Glass calls 'the glitzy mainstream' – at a launch of one of his books in Soho, publicity girls flocking round him as in someone's reverie. He adjourned to a restaurant, where he lifted a finger to the sky, invoked his publisher and assured his guests: 'Nonono! BLOOMZZBURRRAAAAYY! Er, BLOOMZZBURRRAYY will pay, surely? I, er, *I believe they have made some money . . . from a young magician.*'

The episode has a touch of the light fantastic, and of the exotic. There he is, famous, in the thick of Media London, alluding to Harry Potter. But his heart belongs to Glasgow.

To a Glasgow that includes the city of equals pictured in Duncan Thaw's narrative, and in 'the dear green place' of Archie Hind's narrative of that name, which appeared, in all its wealth of detail, fifteen years before *Lanark*, in 1966. Attributions of equality can look chimerical the world over, but the Glasgow of these two friends does seem more equal than most communities. *The Dear Green Place*[48] has tender feelings about a city which is reputed to have little time for such feelings, which has long suffered from high rates of alcoholism, drug use and crime, and continues to deliver some of the worst medical statistics in Europe. Hind's is a tenderness which is quite without the chauvinism that might exploit or forget this, without regard, one way or the other, for matters of reputation. But it's there all right, and can seem to get the better of the irony some might detect in the book's title. He does think of the city as the verdant spot of its Gaelic etymology, as a little poem of his,[49] written for an Edinburgh Festival review, but surely not satirical, might indicate:

> People passing by this way
> Look around then go away
> Never knowing why I say
> Glasgow, the dear green place.

Mat is a slaughterhouse worker who sits up late at home reading and writing, and it's as if his midnight oil has produced – in the teeth of 'the Scotch sneer on his neighbour's face'

– the novel we are now reading. It contains a meditation, out of poverty, on aspiration, on the inevitability of loss and the dissolution of promise, a meditation that turns into the art of its own struggle and insistence, a self-questioning art that is at times barely coherent but at other times moving and winning, an art that is awkward, thrawn and true.

There is another book by Archie Hind which I think is the stronger of the pair. An unfinished novel, no less pledged to aspiration. In *Fur Sadie* a middle-aged Glasgow housewife buys a piano and learns to play it, expecting her venture to be greeted with amusement by her husband and sons. This she receives, together with plenty of vexation and derision. She takes lessons from an overbearing shaggy male genius, McKay, whose showing-off is insufficiently minded by the writer. The work has the power of a central character thoroughly understood and vividly imagined, to a degree that can make the other book seem solipsistic. *Fur Sadie* – a play on the title of the Beethoven piano piece 'Für Elise' – plumbs Sadie's courage and earlier discouragements and straitened expectations. 'It would not be impertinent,' Hinds writes awkwardly, in telling of a shyness of hers, 'to remember here that teeming street, the room-and-kitchen tenement from which Sadie came, her frayed lilac cardigan, nor the street ballads she and other girls sang in the street that summer.' The whole of this fragmentary work is pertinent, whatever risk of sentiment and special pleading may hang about it. Its previously self-effacing life and soul, Sadie, is very endearing; no wonder Alasdair Gray loves her. He calls McKay a 'great teacher', and Sadie's grim marriage a good one, in his introduction, suggesting that she would be likely to have trouble sorting out the males in her life, but that a happy ending may have been planned. Let us hope that it would not have involved an elopement with McKay.

12

CARNIVAL SCOTLAND

Stands Scotland where Irvine Welsh says it does, in his novels *Trainspotting* and *Filth*?[50] It's worth comparing Welsh's fictive Scotland with the less filthy and apparently happier one evoked in the writings of James Hogg, the Ettrick Shepherd, and with the one Hogg appears to have inhabited.

The Scotland Hogg inhabited was no picnic, but was in some respects demonstrably arcadian. He was among the country's early football managers and the job was followed by his presidential commitment to the St Ronan's Border Club, which arranged Games for athletes, anglers and archers. Without having drawn a bow before the age of sixty, Hogg became a champion archer. When the games were over the sportsmen would retire to a convivial supper, where songs were sung, not all of them written and sung by Hogg.

In 1815, together with Walter Scott, he laid on a football game between Yarrow and Selkirk. Scott's son Walter rode onto the field toting the banner of the Buccleuchs. In those days, playing-fields were rarely level, and the opposing sides not necessarily equal in number; some teams could be over a hundred strong. In 1828, Hogg's Ettrick played Yarrow (kickoff 3.15), a game which lasted till darkness fell and ended when the ball was lost. On another occasion Hogg's team lost the game. 'So widely different is theory from practice,' wrote the *Edinburgh Evening Post*.

Hogg loved books, those tile-shaped objects which Welsh professes to abhor, and he loved sport. His sporting life is chronicled in a pamphlet of 1987 by David Groves, 'James Hogg and the St Ronan's Border Club'. In 1824, not long before his Border Olympics was launched, the *Confessions of a Justified Sinner* appeared, with its tennis match, and so, a year later, did his 'epic' poem, *Queen Hynde*, which is in every sense a sport. It's really a satirical extravaganza or Highland Fling. A West Coast Dark Age Scotland of the mind is wildly and sometimes wonderfully projected. A comic-caper Saint Columba is ferried over there from Ulster. He spreads his Christianity – a muscular Christianity as far as his feudal-chieftain allies are concerned – and endeavours to save Caledonia, and its lovely Queen Hynde, from the wrath of the Norseman. This saviour is assisted by a champion who has a more than passing resemblance to James Hogg. Sword fights and Highland games break out. Virgins are fancied, and are due to be raped, burnt alive and sent to Valhalla. In the end, Scotland and Ireland get married. The blood of Fergus – founder of the ancient city of Beregon in present-day Argyllshire – mingles with that of Fingal.

An indeterminancy attends the poem. It can be difficult to tell whether its sympathies are pagan or Christian, popular or patrician. But there's no mistaking the presence of certain of Hogg's ruling passions, just as there's no mistaking the presence of a later Scotland, that of the 1820s. His Albyn or ancient

Caledonia carries the impress of his life and times – of his games and jokes, cronies and causeries, of a conviviality which included the 'Noctes Ambrosianae', conversations scripted by several hands in *Blackwood's Magazine* where a likeness of Hogg gives tongue. His carnival writings, his prose or verse extravaganzas, are drawn to carnage, carnality and cannibalism. No one has ever been more into feasts and galas than Hogg, and in this respect he can be seen as the mediator of a great Scots tradition. This poem, a restored text of which, rid of what are taken to be bowdlerisations, has recently been added to the *Collected Works*, reflects Scotland's devotion to eating and drinking and the maids of Dunedin and elsewhere, to such matters as covens of jolly beggars, balls of Kirriemuir, Tam o' Shanter's night ride, the drunk man's romance with the thistle, to the hallucinated and the surreal, to a literature of wildness and outbreak, much of which the licensing laws have failed to inhibit. It is now time to turn to the writings of Irvine Welsh.

His *Trainspotting* has sport in it. Its circle of drug-users and drinkers cares about rock music and about soccer, though no ghostly team of superstar wasted junkies will ever take the field. None of them could be expected to go kicking balls, or bending bows, after the age of sixty. Its leading figure, Mark Renton, or Rents, who tells most of the story, offers critical severities both on soccer and on music. The novel has sport and conviviality, and carnage – assault and battery, death and faeces – and it also has a kind of ruined carnality.

These features are consonant with what goes on in *Queen Hynde* and in Hogg's phantasmagorias and carnival writings at large. The *Confessions* doesn't belong to the genre, but many of his writings do. Some of them are such as to identify him as the Cannibal King of Scottish Literature, and one of his best stories is about a ravenous shepherd boy and his bid for freedom.[51] Meanwhile, over there in *Trainspotting*, Renton dreams himself on the menu at a cannibal feast.

There are drugs in Welsh's fiction, as we know, and there were drugs in Hogg's world too. The opium-eating De Quincey was a confederate of his at *Blackwood's*. At one point in the 'Noctes Ambrosianae' the Shepherd persona recalls, in highly Hogg-like terms, that he once took laudanum and 'cowped ower', toppled over, and fell asleep for a week. Cowping, so-called, occurs in *Trainspotting*; and Scotland, where the word can also mean screwing in the sexual sense, has its history of cowping in the sense of falling down. It has been prone to proneness. James Boswell was mocked by his English lawyer colleagues, as I love to relate, for 'adhering to the pavement' on circuit, like the spirits in Dante's *Purgatorio*, where prone-ness is described in the language of the Vulgate: *Adhaesit pavimento anima mea*. A description of it in *Trainspotting* reads: 'We left the guy slumped on the pavement.'

There is no close, no narrowly ancestral, relationship between Welsh's works and Hogg's. But there is common ground. There are affinities, which prompt questions about *Trainspotting* and *Filth*, and about the difference between Hogg's merry Scotland and the country evoked by Irvine Welsh, where conviviality has turned sour, where friends are enemies or 'acquaintances', as Renton puts it, and where filth and death play the parts they play in prison camps. Some of the words they use, as I've been suggesting, are significantly the same. Welsh speaks of a 'right motley *ménage à trois*', and 'motley' is a word relished by Hogg which is also a word for much of the work of both writers.

The temptation here is to sentimentalise Hogg's writings, and the world he inhabited. The Scotland of his lifetime had its desperate places, its circles of hell, battalions of the lost, its beggars – 'jakeys', as they are called in *Filth*. Vagrant feasts had already become, in Hogg's day, a topic for writers to be merry about and envious of, as in Burns's celebratory poem, but many of the feasts that actually took place may not have been very different from the liquid ones described in *Trainspotting*. The midnights of the 'resurrectionist' assassins Burke and Hare could be considered a match for what can happen in the Renton circle, with its dead babies and its gangster Begbie. All the same, while 'Scotland' may be too compendious a concept for it to make perfect sense to compare past and present embodiments in search of a change for better or worse, it is possible to feel that the idea of progress in which people used to believe would encourage no one to prefer Welsh's Leith to Hogg's Innerleithen.

Reread five years after its appearance in 1993, *Trainspotting* seems, more than ever, a talented and adventurous book. It is as funny as it is harrowing. Its argot is rich in invention, authorial and tribal – 'weedjies' for Glaswegians, and so on. Rhyming slang works well in both novels. In *Trainspotting*, the command of vernacular Scots contends with Hogg's; and both men can move to a seamless, simultaneous Scots and English. Here, complaining of the heat, goes Renton's friend the hippy-innocent Murphy (with his distinctive and compulsive 'likesay', Edinburgh's answer to 'as it were'):

The Fit ay Leith Walk is really likes, mobbed oot man. It's too hot for a fair-skinned punter, likesay, ken? Some cats thrive in the heat, but the likes ay me, ken, we jist cannae handle it. Too severe a gig man.

I can sympathise with those who are upset by the book, who can't bear its zestful descriptions of cruel acts, who think of it as punk-fashionable, as an accession to the culture of disgust, or as a sick joke. The chapter which has the assault on the dying Venters – by means of a simulated child abuse – is certainly more or less unbearable, whether read as a piece of punk camp, or punk chic, or as a forced or contrived assault on tender sensibilities, delivered at a time when the exposure of child abuse is more prominent in this society than it has been in the past. My own renewed experience of *Trainspotting*, nevertheless, is of a book which is both impressive and appealing.

It's a series of loosely related stories, as one or two of Hogg's books are. It can appear confused, though it's also true to say that, like Hogg's *Confessions*, it can appear more confused than it really is. It features two wakes, and two disgraceful male awakenings at the house of a girl's parents – this might seem careless; and the account of the Venters revenge might seem insufficiently careless, might seem designing. Despite all this, *Trainspotting* does not register as an ephemeral or opportunistic book.

There were early readers who felt that it was far too user-friendly, that Welsh was out to celebrate his addicts – the authorially-embraced Renton above all – and to side with them in their encounters with specimens of a diabolic-pathetic middle class or mainstream. Renton's hatred goes out to the whole damned lot of shoppers, voters, viewers, tourists, elderly relatives, all those people who could be perceived as the financers of his habit. Edinburgh's punters and wankers are blamed for watching the junk television watched by the junkies themselves. But it's also the case that the novel is replete with instances of addict misery and mortality, and with Renton's various but seldom self-flattering explanations of why people take drugs, and that it offers kind thoughts and improving reflections which can only be read as reflecting on the behaviour of its users. None of this deserves to be overlooked – though it has to be admitted that there's some effect of incongruity here. More readers must surely have warmed to the novel for its wit, and for the sympathy it extends to some of its users, than for its cautionary notes.

Renton's socialist sermons are subject to uncertainty; Murphy wonders whether he means these sermons. They can nevertheless be eloquent. One riff was apparently adopted for propaganda purposes by a risk-taking Scottish National Party intellectual:

Ah don't hate the English. They're just wankers. We are colonised by wankers. We can't even pick a decent, vibrant, healthy culture to be colonised by. No. We're ruled by effete arseholes. What does that make us? The lowest of the fuckin low, the scum of the earth. The most wretched, servile, miserable, pathetic trash that was ever shat intae creation. Ah don't hate the English. They just git oan wi the shite thuv goat. Ah hate the Scots.

'Scotland takes drugs in psychic self-defence,' runs one of the novel's explanations. Against what? The English are down there getting on with the shite they've got, and despite having operated in the north of the island as a colonial power, as Renton believes, they aren't represented in the book as posing a threat. Renton even has English friends, and has joined them in a cross-border dole scam. 'Against Scotland' would seem to be the answer. He makes it plain elsewhere, incidentally, that countries, all countries, disgust him; we are nowhere told if any of them possess healthy cultures.

Renton's opinions display the aggression that Scots people have a reputation for displaying. He is neither an Anglophobe nor a Scottish Nationalist, and is relatively humane about women. But he is fierce about much else, about careerists and conformists, and with reference to such sporting matters as Hearts versus Hibs (he is a Hibbie who hates Jambos – a name that plays on 'tarts' and on the Stallone *nom de guerre*). He is fierce enough, and firm enough, to take the money and run from his friends. None of this, however, makes this verbal militant a hard man, any more than it makes his opinions uninteresting. The novel hints that he is a 'closet-sap', and he has been construed as a secret reader, addicted to books as well as to drugs. Relish the thought that the man we see breasting the fecal tide of a jakes in search of smack suppositories might at some other point be detected on the beach reading Kierkegaard or Kafka.

Are we to think that *Trainspotting* is what happens when a Caledonian gloom meets the Kierkegaardian uncertainty which Renton or his writer has discovered in a book, and which is seen here, in Existentialist fashion, as a basis for choice or decision? Kierkegaard's contemporary, Hogg, lit on his own principle of uncertainty in the *Confessions*, and it may not be outlandish to claim a further affinity, in this regard, between Welsh and his predecessor. Each of these books builds on the uncertainties, the complexities, of its writer, and the resemblance between Renton and his writer reflects this. Welsh has in his time been a man of business, an investor, a realtor, and he came to be called, on occasion, 'the millionaire from Muirhouse'. It's hard to imagine Rents in real estate. Or is it?

Renton refers – in the words of Keats – to 'the misery ay the world'. He holds that 'life's boring and futile': 'we live a short, disappointing life; and then we die. We fill up oor lives wi shite, things like careers and relationships . . .' We never get far with knowing 'about the big things'. He praises smack for its simplicity. 'Yuv just goat one thing tae worry aboot,' when you're on drugs. But he then has to concede that smack wastes you and is no life at all. Smack ensures that while he and his mates flinch from Begbie, they are unable to restrain his violence: 'We played a big part in making him what he was.'

Welsh takes pleasure in violence at times, as does Hogg at times, with both of them meanwhile disapproving of it: Hogg's collection of 'Lay Sermons' proclaims this disapproval. Begbie speaks of the 'rules ay the game', one of which enjoins punching the woman who is carrying your child if she screams at you. The novelist is obviously not in favour of that.

Francis Begbie fleetingly appears in *Filth*, where the narrator, Bruce Robertson, also speaks about the rules of the game. Begbie is mostly seen through Renton's hostile eyes in the earlier novel, whereas in the later one the consciousness of its even-worse-than-Begbie Robertson presides. The later novel contains a murder-mystery, somewhat mechanically resolved, which matters less to the reader than this consciousness, the narrator's, as it plays on the departure of a wife and child, on promotion prospects and on the cars, hash, booze, crimes and graft of a Los Angeles-like city life. A citizen of, in fact, Edinburgh, Bruce is a detective, and a not wholly detestable comic dynamo who unloads a voracious and anthropophagous delirium – of oral and other sex, junk food, treachery and mayhem. The stories he tells of himself are almost all unequivocally unflattering. Serving as a strike-breaking policeman against Arthur Scargill's miners is scarcely the worst of these stories. His doing so may give an inkling of the writer's politics, as may the attack on the absentee-chauvinist film-star Sean Connery: 'Come back for ten minutes tae tell the daft cunts that they need a parliament, but dinnae stick around long enough tae vote in it!' The *Los Angeles Times* has mentioned this narrator's 'indeterminacy', and might have done the same for Renton. Renton and Robertson and Welsh could all be called in different degrees undecidable.

A tape-worm resident in his intestines conveys that Robertson, the abuser and tormenter, was himself abused and tormented when he was young. Part of his police work has been called a response to the activities of Ian Rankin's fictional Edinburgh detective, Rebus; the delirium may also be indebted to the carnival nightmares of the American novelists James Ellroy (investigator of his mother's murder, confessor of his juvenile delinquencies) and Carl Hiaasen. A debt to Hogg, and resemblances to Hogg, are hardly prominent here.

Robertson keeps saying: 'Same rules apply.' The mantra can seem to mean what Begbie means by such talk. Implied, too, is a Masonic solidarity: Robertson is a member of that brotherhood, which is pictured as a conspiracy aimed at Papist Scotland. The mantra can mean that folk are weak, and rotten laws better than none. Elsewhere it can mean anarchy and a manipulation of the weak.

Some readers might feel that Welsh enjoys the bad things done by Robertson, while tending to disown them by rendering them so little excusable. Robertson extracts sex from a posh girl whose father is an obnoxious barrister who gets criminals off: it's the price she must pay for not being framed for a drug offence. 'The Leith police dismisseth us' is a saying with which no one who grew up in Midlothian is unfamiliar: this episode makes it seem that much more sinister. At another point, he dismisseth, as unfit to talk to, the 'uniformed spastics' of the Leith constabulary.

Welsh, who used to say that the book was dead, has since said that *Filth* may be his last.[52] It is not the book that *Trainspotting* is. Marlowe's demonic Jew of Malta tells the audience what they want to hear about how he goes around a-poisoning wells: without the sanction of Elizabethan stage convention, Robertson's clean breast outdoes the Jew of Malta and pushes at the preposterous. But the driving grunginess and genuine passion of passages like the one in which he tells of going around a-poisoned by a pubic eczema are impossible to wave away, as show-off hyperbole.

I grew up in Midlothian, near where Welsh once lived for a time, and where the autobiographical film-maker Bill Douglas grew up. Welsh's Muirhouse is a mile or two from my mining village of Gilmerton. We were close, too, to the estate, or scheme, of Craigmillar, where the 'schemie blood' sneered at by Robertson was a fighting force and a byword for wildness in the Forties, and where the needle then took over, toppling its aggressives, giving rise to rumours of dereliction. It will be a long time, though, before it wipes out the native vigour of the place. One local man is reported to have been lively enough to come up to Welsh, who was filming on the estate, and ask for a cut of the profits from his literary efforts, in view of the contribution to his art made by this man and his pals.

Gilmerton figures in a surreal television play of his as a place where the vibes are bad and work is gone, and the old folk sit around in their bungalows diverting themselves with dildoes, while a bevvying God sits in the pub being sardonic. Gilmerton has changed since I lived there – the pit has closed and the pub is wider open – and Welsh's play deliriously distorts its current state. It has been drowned in jokes.

My memories of the village include events at its primary school, where, for the nine-year-olds, 'the top of the class' was a desk in the far corner of the last row at the end. I aspired to squeeze into that desk, and I had a rival in a girl whose jotter I looked at. I found an essay of hers in which were the words: 'It smelled for all the world like chrysanthemums.' 'What style,' I jealously thought. And I still think it a good sentence. Margaret, who became a nurse, was one of the interesting people, young and old, who lived in the neighbourhood. Welsh's village does not smell of chrysanthemums. There are people in the village now who are like the interesting people who were around there seventy years ago, but Welsh's Gilmerton has to exclude them. This is not to protest that it's all a fabrication.

13

LORD DACRE
HAMMERS THE SCOTS

One way of discovering whether or not you love your native country, in my case Scotland, is to read a book by a writer you admire which runs the country down. I am an Anglo-Scot with an interest in Scottish literature who has spent most of his working life in London, and I am largely an enemy of nationalism. In the eyes, therefore, of the sizable minority of Scots who are thought to favour a break with England I'm hardly the right person to be tendering my affectionate respects, as I now nevertheless do.

The history of relations between the Nationalist leadership in the North and successive Westminster governments is no great argument for devolution. But devolution has shown itself capable of development, and it strikes me as better than a break, better than behaving as the separate half of a small and struggling island at a time when many nations are doing badly. The late English historian Hugh Trevor-Roper was opposed to a Scottish separation, and his posthumously assembled book, *The Invention of Scotland*, was composed at a time when the country's future was being re-invented. He felt that a united Scotland, England and Wales would be 'more progressive in character', as his present editor has expressed it, than any of them would be by itself.[53] But his concern was not that of a man who loved Scotland. 'As a general rule I can do without the Scots,' he told a correspondent once. The romantic Cavalier general Montrose, poet and political ally of the Anglo-Scottish poet William Drummond of Hawthornden, belonged, he claimed, to an 'exquisite generation' which 'contrived to produce a poet even in Scotland – the last poet ever to arise in that prosaic peninsula'.

He claimed, moreover, that it was natural that 18th-century Scots, 'seeking compensation for the end of their independent history and politics, should turn to discover and appreciate their native literature. Unfortunately, when they looked for it, they could not find it. There was none.' The cupboard was bare. Scotland had never had a literature, and it was not about to have a poetry. As for England's Stuart dynasty, they were spivs. 'Those feckless Scottish kings'![54] This gifted historian, myth-hater and militant rationalist did not love Scotland, but he was mad about it – in the sense that he had an urge to tease and torment it, to invent for it a charge sheet of faults and deficiencies which can sometimes seem like a myth of his own.

'My ambition is to solve intellectual problems and present my solutions in satisfying aesthetic form,' he declared.[55] This was an ambition calculated to upset those historians for whom good writing and artistic effect are disqualifying, and it was one which was fulfilled. He was a good writer and a concise and witty narrator with an eye for character and for irony and idiosyncrasy, who also set himself to generalise and to function as a social historian. His tradition was that of Tacitus and Gibbon, and his most successful medium, if we discount his excellent letters, was the essay. Collected in his *Historical Essays*, the account of Erasmus, and of the ironies of his responsibility for the Reformation, is, I think, among his finest performances. His principal stamping-ground was the politics, ecclesiastics and Hermetics of the Early Modern period.

Trevor-Roper, having become Lord Dacre, died in 2003. His new book is an old one. Parts of it have appeared before in early versions – Chapters 7 and 8 come from a collection of essays by several hands, *The Invention of Tradition* of 1983, and most of the writing appears to have been done over the interval 1979–81. Brilliantly iconoclastic at its best, the book falls into three episodes, featuring the mythic history produced by George Buchanan, the contested poetry of James Macpherson's *Ossian* and the cult of the kilt. Pre-Ossianic 'Scottish culture had always been sustained by forgery,' he writes:[56] he had a lifelong interest in forgery, and the prosecutorial approach evident in his treatment of these episodes is far from infrequent elsewhere. The Trevor-Roper tribunal is often in session, icons are clattered. These were to include Arnold Toynbee's *Study of History*, and the doctrines that Puritanism (and indeed Judaism) and capitalism were closely aligned, and that industrial capitalism began in the 17th century.

There's more, of course, to Scotland's faults, as he sees them, than forgery and susceptibility to myth. 'The Picts, as light-minded as they were light-fingered, drove their former friends clean out of the country and back into Ireland': such expulsions are not usually a project of light minds and light fingers. 'The generosity of Highlanders has seldom been expressed in cash,' he writes, with reference to the finances of the Highland

Society of London, and to a time in the 1780s when 'Ossian' Macpherson was serving at home as godfather to a Highland 'mafia', as Trevor-Roper calls it, ensconced in India, who were well prepared to express their mutual generosity in cash.[57]

The first of the three episodes is about a leading Latin poet of the Renaissance, and a historian of influence, whose work has long been known as in part apocryphal. Much is made of Buchanan's dependence on Boece and other fabulists, and of the resultant notion of hundreds of years of Scottish prehistory, with a line of no less than forty kings. Buchanan was to argue a thesis in defence of the deposition of tyrannical kings by their nobility, a thesis which circulated in samizdat after its banning by James VI, and was to be perceived as republican in tendency. Scottish kings had been deposed in the past, as Shakespeare's *Macbeth* was soon to show, without offering itself as a republican or democratic vehicle; and a Scottish queen and a Scottish king were presently to be deposed and executed. Buchanan's position is represented by Trevor-Roper as an archetypal 'whig' interpretation of the past. He sees Buchanan as a man of secular mind, and thinks that the view of him as a Protestant hero is untenable. He was nonetheless a vehement anti-Papist and anti-Franciscan, and Robert Crawford has lately spoken of his 'remarkable elegy for Jean Calvin'.[58] It would be possible to imagine a less forensic or inculpatory account of Buchanan than the one that figures in these sprightly chapters.

And so to 'the broken poems of Ossian', James Macpherson's lyrical versions of alleged fragments of ancient Gaelic poetry which surfaced in 1760, and were seized on by Scots anxious for wur 'Epics' to be restored, and then by *tout Paris*, Europe and America, but which were to be challenged – by Samuel Johnson and by a line of Scottish scholars from Malcolm Laing to Derick Thomson in the 1950s. Ossian, bardic son of the warrior Fingal, was an impersonation by James Macpherson, aided by manuscript and transcript material which he shielded from subsequent enquiry. These chapters were drafted in the early Eighties. Fiona Stafford's instructive study of 1988, *The Sublime Savage*, appears only in the editor's guide to Further Reading, where it is put down with a 'stronger on empathetic understanding than on judgment' – perhaps she was judged too kind to the culprit. Living Gaelic poets of the 18th century – Rob Donn, William Ross and Duncan Ban MacIntyre – are not discussed in the book.

The Ossian poems affect most readers now, I gather, as an uncrossable post-Jacobite prairie of grief and chief, courage and carnage, downfall and nightfall, as promising, without delivering, an escape from the 18th-century parlour. Macpherson was not long in giving up poetry for politics and British Empire hustling, but in the meantime, covered in girls and ornaments, he had become a celebrity. Boswell told of a meeting with this 'Sublime Savage' and of his dislike of Gray's Sassenach Elegy: '"Hoot!" cried Fingal, "to write panegyrics upon a parcel of damned rogues that did nothing but plough the land and saw corn!"' Macpherson was a more martial figure than Robert Burns, apparently. David Hume told of him: 'He would have all the Nation divided into Clans, and these clans to be always fighting.'[59] A reference, presumably, to Hume's native Scotland.

The most welcome contributions made in Trevor-Roper's book to the Macpherson story are the strong case it pursues for the participation in *Ossian* of a clansman of his, Lachlan Macpherson, laird of Strathmashie, Gaelic poet and scholar, and the role played in the questioning of the work by the distinguished and enraged historian, despiser of Celts and Highlanders and forger of old ballads, John Pinkerton. Pinkerton was a friend and questioner of James Hogg, whose Dark Age Scotland mock-epic *Queen Hynde*, a Lowland peasant's Celt-centred cosmogony, was published in 1825. A Scots-Irish Caledonia, the land of Fingal and Fergus and a pugnacious Saint Columba, is revealed here. This is the terrain of the Ossian pieces, and its capital city of Beregon is mentioned by Trevor-Roper. But *Queen Hynde* is not. Hogg said he believed in *Ossian*, and he was influenced by it. He also felt he'd out-Ossianed Macpherson in Scotland.[60] In many of these activities a period element of play should be acknowledged. Tricks were being played – even by Sir Walter Scott.

It sometimes looks as if Trevor-Roper's book is more interested in the forensic than in the literary aspect of the Ossian tricks. But he is not without sympathy with his author. 'If we assume that Macpherson had based his Ossian not on the old manuscripts, which he could not read, but on an intermediate Gaelic text, whose relationship to those manuscripts was unverifiable by him, then his difficulty becomes clear.' And if we assume that there is merit in the hypothesis that he had 'accomplices', then it serves to reduce 'the charge against the principal accused . . . from machiavellian fraud to lower and more human proportions'.[61] He does not spell out what these proportions are, and he does not go into the question of what Macpherson et al. were trying to achieve and why for a while it succeeded so luxuriantly, in a manner that can bring to mind the aura that surrounded the poetry of Gaeldom's Dylan Thomas in the 1940s. A Celtic twilight descended, and lingered for more than a hundred years, and many a lost soul wandered there.

Role-playing and imposture were activities with which the literature of that modern world was complicit. Scott and Hogg lent their lines to the transmission of the great Border Ballads, and Hogg was reported as boasting that he'd taken Wattie in with his inventions when it came to writing the ballads down. To speak of 'corruption', as has constantly been done in the case both of the ballads and of Ossian, is a pious error and hyperbole (Macpherson himself was known to complain of the corruption that had tainted his sources). The hidden hand of the collaborator and concealed author did much for the Scottish literary tradition among others, and was superbly brandished in the first phase of *Blackwood's Magazine*.

Such was Scott's status that it was forgotten, or forgiven, that the Great Unknown of the Waverley novels belonged in this capacity to a culture of economies with the truth, imperfect disclosure, constructive clandestinity. Hogg was one of the few who has ever called the great man a cheat over the lies he admitted to over the Waverley authorship. Copying, imitation, pseudonymity, anonymity were as common then as they have ever been anywhere. Meanwhile the myths of which nations are made have been common too, all over the place. The Scots are not uniquely credulous. Trevor-Roper's disapproval of myth ran deep but could at times be suspended, just as his disapproval of religion was not unqualified: 'A world without devotion seems to me arrogant and vulgar, a world without myth mean and threadbare.'[62] For all the assertions of one or two of his enemies, he had a heart.

On the book moves to the wearing of the kilt, which is not the ancient article that some, but surely not many, may still suppose. It is dated to a point between the Jacobite rebellions, and is said to have been invented by an English Quaker. Highland dress was forbidden after the Forty-Five: any man or boy caught wearing 'plaid, philibeg, trews, shoulder-belts ... tartans or parti-coloured plaid or stuff'[63] was liable by statute to be jailed or transported. The valour of George III's Highland soldiers, and the festivities, organised by Scott, for George IV's visit to Edinburgh in 1825, monstrously philibegged and tighted, said goodbye to all that. A Celtification of Scotland was devised on this occasion: Highland chiefs surged with their tails of retainers to Holyrood. The occasion has served as a topos for several writers since. Trevor-Roper takes, and does, his turn on the subject.

He remarks that Macaulay, of Highland stock, one of his favourite historians, was 'powerless' against the fallacy of Celtification. On the facing page is a sharp passage from Macaulay which blames the fallacy on Trevor-Roper's equally admired Walter Scott, and in which he writes with irony about a flourishing of plaid and claymore: 'by most Englishmen, Scotchman and Highlander were regarded as synonymous words.' Tartan is clearly a tricky subject. A hundred and seventy-five years before the Holyrood shindig Andrew Marvell celebrated Cromwell's triumphant return from Ireland:

> The Pict no shelter now shall find
> Within his party-colour'd mind,

But from this valour sad
Shrink underneath the plad.

He seems to be speaking of an ur-tartan garment in these compacted lines. Scott is quoted as saying that 'the general proposition that the Lowlanders ever wore plaids is difficult to swallow.'[64] Had he answered the front-door bell at Abbotsford, he might have found before him his neighbour Hogg, the Ettrick Shepherd, clad in a parti-coloured plaid. These are engrossing chapters. They end with an account of the Sobiesky Stuarts, two English brothers who claimed royal blood. One of them engaged in a serious history of Highland costume.

The Invention of Scotland is locally rewarding, but it can't, broadly speaking, be described as innovatory. When I was an adolescent in Midlothian, I knew that *Ossian* was an 18th-century poem, knew of its doubtful provenance, and felt that I might never be able to read it through. The little I knew of George Buchanan is likely to have included a sense that his history was partly apocryphal. I wore a Buchanan kilt on Sundays back then, no doubt of doubtful provenance, but I grew to mind the palaver about tartan, like others I knew, and like Billy Connolly. I remember walking by the Firth of Forth with a friend who observed: 'There's a man in a kilt. He must be English.' He wore a kilt himself in adult life, of unexampled gravity – as if to shame me as I went around, now and then, in my vivacious Buchanan tie. My grandmother's middle name was Buchan, you see. I wore it for her. Fergus was a middle name of mine (a leader's name from the traditions of the Gael, *vide* Fergus I of Scotland).

Trevor-Roper was a controversial figure. Why, it was asked, was he so hostile? Historians, faced with their various uncertainties, often talk of the need to get things right, but this historian's appetite for authentication, for the detection of fraud and unreason, must at times have been experienced as acute. The appetite was punished by the irony of his temporary mis-authentication of the faked Hitler diaries: when he died, most newspapers confined their attention to this error and gave none to his performance as a historian. These concerns of his are reflected in his too often thrilled and deferential letters to the grand authenticator, the Jewish American art-dealer-advising art historian Bernard Berenson, in his Florentine villa of I Tatti, where at three in the afternoon precisely he would descend a staircase to greet a throng of rapt visitors. Trevor-Roper was a democrat of sorts: he seems to have believed with Machiavelli that aristocracies 'may preserve themselves longest', as he paraphrased the position, 'but only democracies, which refresh their ruling class, can expand'.[65] He was also, he said, a snob. He didn't care for the 'opulence' of James I's London court, but was ready to admit elsewhere that he liked 'the world of grace and leisure, and the opulence necessary to maintain it'.[66] I Tatti monitored that world.

Lord Dacre hammers the Scots – why, in particular, was he so down on *them*? The son of a cold country doctor, reportedly, he was raised on the English side of the border with Scotland, and as with English-hating Hugh MacDiarmid, who was raised to the west on the other side, a breath of feud and of the auld enemy may have blown about his ears. Here were two frontiersmen, each intent on his game or half-game of hating the other side. Here, perhaps, was the exacerbated sense of identity which has been spotted in borderers. Trevor-Roper's present editor conveys that his nanny, governess and wife were Scotch – the form Trevor-Roper preferred, in part at least for historical reasons; and he had a house, Chiefswood, in the Scotch Borders, where I remember him starting from the undergrowth of his garden, a rake rather than a pen in his hot hand, looking faintly like Fingal. He was otherwise austerely spruce – officer material, Prussian Officer material (Intelligence branch) at moments.

His translation to the old Oxford of snobbery and spite can hardly have tempered his capacity for hostility or his aversion to the Scots. For a specimen of that Oxford see his colleague Maurice Bowra's letter of 1947 to Evelyn Waugh, who would have known about Trevor-Roper's aversion to the Catholic Church:

> Trevor-Roper is a fearful man, short-sighted, with dripping eyes, shows off all the time, sucks up to me, boasts, is far from poor owing to his awful book, on every page of which there is a howler.[67]

This seems like a sucking-up to the supremely hostile Waugh – and it's no doubt conceivable that Bowra and Trevor-Roper were on some other occasions friends. The book referred to was *The Last Days of Hitler*, published in the early days of Trevor-Roper.

I was a friend of his myself, and we got on very well together when he wrote for journals I edited. I felt for him what I felt for Scotland: my fondness for him, that's to say, had a touch of the adversarial. It was sauced by an awareness of our differences of outlook, by my wariness of his Oxford grandeur, by his disapproval of some of my compatriots, and by my disapproval of the opulent Berenson. Another memory I have of him is of standing with him on the Mound in Edinburgh, on our way down from the National Library, and going on about the pre-Holocaust anti-semitism of a certain writer. He replied that those were different days. He was right to say this, and I was right to feel that no days are different when it comes to that sort of thing. He himself was philo-semitic. He was willing to call Erasmus an anti-semite, despite his Jewish supporters and interpreters, but he wasn't one himself. He did not say to me what Boswell said to Johnson, that I could not help being Scottish, and he did not say that I couldn't help being base-born. I think I would have noticed. He really was what is often called, sometimes fulsomely, a good friend. I take pleasure in the conviction that his work as a historian – especially the 17th-century work which began with Archbishop Laud and ended with the posthumous book on the Hermetic Huguenot physician Thomas de Maherne – will last.

A nation's characteristics are, like dreams, 'aye contrary' – full of contradiction. The Scots are friendly, decent, less snobbish than the English. They were Thatcher-proof. They are also immemorially fierce. The *perfervidum ingenium Scotorum* has been hostile to strangers. It was hard to miss what Irvine Welsh must have meant when he recently and contentiously declared that Hugh MacDiarmid embodied the worst faults of the Scottish male. Or what Celtic Andrew O'Hagan meant by his blast of the trumpet (resented and avenged, and now reproduced in a gathering of his essays) about a Scottish commitment to self-pity, nostalgia, xenophobia, self-righteous blame.[68] This native hostility is a weariness of the Ossian poems, and it would not be an asset for any separate Scotland that may transpire. Scotland has always been a parti-coloured place, as opposed to a blood-brotherhood, and the same is true of Britain, which could and should continue to house the gallimaufry of its northern end. Let's not be Balkans. Let's not, in Hume's words, have all the nation divided into clans, and these clans to be always fighting. Robert Burns could be angry, with plenty to be angry about. But he did not, as far as I can tell, 'hate the English'.

Violence, fervour – 'passion' in MacDiarmid-speak – they have their contradictions, their compulsions, their compunctions, their boasts. These are visible in Gregory Burke's balletic *Black Watch*, which has carried to the stage the testimonies of soldiers from the regiment of that name. The Iraq war is seen from the point of view of the platoon, the regiment, the clan. *Black Watch*, with its dark tartan and its red hackles, is one of modern Scotland's more resonant works of art. A 'Highland' regiment dominated by its Lowland intakes, the Black Watch fought fiercely for the London-based British Empire; and at about the time it was taking casualties in Iraq it was merged with a larger formation of the Anglo-Scottish Army. Clans have their famous victories, but they don't win all their wars.

14

EPILIMNION RE-USED

Soviet policemen once asked a woman where she kept her jewels, and she is said to have replied: 'I am the only jewel in this house.' Candia McWilliam is the precious stone of her memoir, a self-orphaned orphan's delirium.[69] She, too, has been interrogated – by her native city's more hidebound and respectable faubourgs, bent on asking of the authoress, so to speak, 'What kind of name is *that*, for heaven's sake?'; and by book-reviewers bent on complaining of stylistic exaggeration and on accusing her of having swallowed a dictionary. To the inkhorn charge among others, *What to Look for in Winter* has apt replies, reminiscent of that of the Soviet suspect.

She was born and reared in Edinburgh, and belonged to the city's often English-speaking upper class, which was not without its indigenous and its bohemian tendencies. Her mother committed suicide when Candia was young, and she later left her father's house for that of a surrogate family, the Howards, on the West Coast island of Colonsay. This was not her only 'cuckooing', as she calls it. She was also looked after by the Mitchison clan in Edinburgh, by the mother in particular, Rosalind, English author of the best history of Scotland known to the present writer. She went to Cambridge, where she rattled the sherry glasses of Girton, and then to the very fruitful *Vogue* academy of aspirant female writers.

Her fiction began in 1988, and came to a halt in 1997. She married a titled landowner by whom she had two children, and left him for a 'beautiful' Parsee Oxford academic for whom the word 'don' might have been invented: Fram Dinshaw possessed 'a cool distaste for weakness'. She left Dinshaw too, by whom she had a son, but kept up with both ex-husbands and with their respective second partners. Her experience of the extended family can be considered extensive. All of these people, former spouses and new partners, seem to have helped her remarkably with the difficulties that overtook her, halted her. She had become an alcoholic, eventually escaping through an approximation to AA attendance, and in 2006 she became effectively blind with the onset of the rare condition blepharospasm, whereby the eyelids refuse to open: she had to hold hers open manually in order to catch glimpses of the world. The earlier parts of her autobiography were dictated.

After much consulting, physiological and psychological, orthodox and occult, a friend and fellow-sufferer put her on to a doctor who had successfully treated the condition by taking tendons from the back of the leg and grafting them onto the area of the eye. The sick are unlikely to be cheered by the thought that a line of eminent medical men had preceded the lucky chance of an introduction to someone who knew what to do. She can now see, and she can now compose, after a long spell of drought, signalled, as it might seem, by the loss of her sight.

She sees herself as accident-prone and error-prone, and at fault. Images of the witch, and of the 'beloved monster', come and go in the memoir. She is 'gullible'. She has fits and falls. She sets herself on fire. She has been deemed a word-addict. And a bolter. She calls herself a shape-changer; and at an earlier point seems to have borne a version of the first name of her second husband's second partner. Her life is portrayed as careering, wandering, bewildered. It's a life in which 'nimiety' – a dictionary word for excess, applied to her by her second husband – is pitted against utility or practicality. And yet this *mea culpa* carries a strong sense of Candia McWilliam's grasp of her own nature. Her faults can be experienced as contributions to the picture of a vivid and rewarding idiosyncrasy.

The book's wandering quality, its taste for uncertainty, shows itself in relation to this business of her word-love. Its words can occasionally give pause. Not all of such words suggest dictation in a darkened room; an old propensity of hers may be in evidence. She mentions bouts of parental fighting: 'There was some scuffing.' Scuffling, perhaps? Well, no: there's a figurative reference to shoes here. Soon afterwards we learn that her grandfather called her mother 'Scruff'. These two s-words could perhaps be thought to be responding to one another. She writes of the inkhorn term 'epilimnion': 'I even wake up saying it. This may be a bad case of "Candia McWilliam's swallowed the dictionary", because I've only the slightest idea of what it means, which is, I think, the top surface of a large body of water, for example a lake. What I don't know is how many meniscuses make up an epilimnion.' She proceeds to re-use the word, which is absent from the *Oxford English Dictionary*. She does this both in its putative sense and in others, and she does so to great effect. Some of its vagaries add to the startling gaiety of the memoir.

This is a romantic work, not least because of its cultivation of uncertainty and ambiguity, its interest in Rabelais's 'great perhaps', to which it refers. Multiple personality, the individual's quarrelling selves – 'That's me.' She is the self-felling tree which isn't dead yet. She is both 'performative and shy'. She is both tall and short, fat and thin, successively or otherwise. To be in charge, or not in charge, of several selves or shapes is not to cease to be a recognisable person or a convincing fictional character. Candia McWilliam is very much there in her memoir, in the role of its diamond departer and whitish witch.

She loves and praises people a lot. 'There has to be nothing she cannot do,' she writes, with a touch of nimiety, about a fine schoolteacher. She has a feeling for Scotland: but I've heard the book described as cod-Scottish. I don't believe that this is the case. Gentry Scots are given to coming on as Scots, while also alluding to compatriots as Jocks. She is no performing Scot, but is nevertheless ('niverthelace', in Muriel Spark's specimen of Edinburgh speech) the living breath of a cosmopolitan Anglo-Scotswoman with a braw gift for words, a Stevensonian and therefore sufficiently Scottish phenomenon. It is impossible to read her book without consciousness of the suffering she has endured and now commemorates. But she does not need you to keep thinking it courageous.

15

GULLEYING ABOUT

The young Philip Larkin was keen on the writings of D.H. Lawrence. Perhaps more surprisingly, he was also keen on another enemy of the bourgeoisie, Joyce Cary's rogue painter Gulley Jimson in the novel *The Horse's Mouth*, which appeared in 1944. Larkin relished the spectacle of the old sod painting away on the run from the police, dangling from the heights of a ruined Thames-side chapel, struggling with a mural devoted to 'the Creation'. Jimson has been based by rumour on Stanley Spencer, but there have been other contenders for his original, and there were many at the time who wanted to sit for the portrait. This was, and has remained, an influential book.

It may be that Larkin's enthusiasm for Jimson did not survive the rigours of the Movement outlook, with its aversion to demonstrative genius, and it would seem that Cary's reputation has paled since his death in 1957. A winning streak has been ascribed to the work he did during the Second World War and on its eve. *The Horse's Mouth* and *Mister Johnson*, which preceded it in 1939, are his best-known books. He was, however, a copious and various writer, and it is good that his merits have been restored to notice by the inclusion of nine of his novels in the Faber Finds series of reprints.[70]

Cary was born in Derry in Ireland in 1888 of ancient landed stock, due to be dispossessed of its estates; his grandmother went to live in a cottage near Castle Cary. He studied art and served in West Africa as a soldier, against the Germans, and as a district officer. Wounded at the battle of Mount Mora in 1916. After the war he settled in Oxford.

'I detest allegory,' he said: 'my people are real people in a real world or they are nothing.' The philosophical statements made in his novels are certainly less persuasive than his people. He believes in freedom and creativity, as many people do. Freedom is associated with creativity and is distinguished from liberty, seen as an absence of constraint. The distinction might be compared with the one on liberty argued by Isaiah Berlin – an Oxford matter, this, as the distinction might conceivably seem. Cary can be said to look both forward and back. His fiction follows the fortunes of the Liberal Party of his early days, and his words recall the complications of its origins, the watchword of advocates of the 1832 Reform Bill – Macaulay's 'Reform that you may preserve.'

Freedom and creativity are also associated with delinquency. The creative, the free, misbehave, with Jimson as culprit-in-chief. Elsewhere Cary's Mister Johnson is an African clerk, an honorary Englishman and a species of black-and-white minstrel. He pilfers and confusedly kills, requests and receives a bullet in the head from the district officer he loves, is given to music and dancing and verse impromptus, does his bit for the British Empire, and is, like Mister Jimson, if less operatically, a type of the artist.

The year after *Mister Johnson*, the boy thief Charley in *Charley is My Darling* was awarded the name of artist. He takes things, draws things, Gulleys about. He is 'special'. Geniuses are mocked in the novel, but Charley is suspected of being one, and he has the larcenies to show for it. He dices with the prison cell that awaits Cary's artists, while showing the imaginative flair expected of artists at large. The novel itself has this flair. It was enterprising of Cary to go among schoolchildren in this wholehearted way. A decade before Golding's *Lord of the Flies*, Charley heads a gang of evacuees cast away, as it can seem, in a mostly hostile English countryside. The novel owes less to its series of strangely undetected burglaries than it does to Charley's relations with his girlfriend and with the kind woman in nominal charge of the evacuees, whose trust in him is sorely tested.

Slaps, biffs and bruises are rife in Cary's fiction of the 1940s, which saw, on the home front, some of the great days of authoritarian violence, parents against children, masters against servants, husbands against wives. Jimson beats his women like the drums Johnson likes to listen to, while trading his own blows in the Bush. *Mister Johnson* is a very funny book which is now bound to appear politically incorrect. The district officer's wife refers to the clerk, in semi-friendly style, as Mr Wog, and if this seems condescending, so quite often does the novel. The charming clerk can even seem soft in the head, the village idiot. There's a feeling here, nonetheless, for the political freedom that was later to blow through Africa, and the account of the British Empire is far from indulgent. The bureaucracy of its outposts – roads, taxes, petty cash and its disappearance – is made wholly convincing.

Gulley Jimson is the supreme menace of these three characters, and the threat he represents is proportioned to the sense we may be meant to have that he is a genius and that the paintings he does are worth stealing for. His masterpieces – more like Chagall, perhaps, than anyone else – are to be taken seriously, and the novel is haunted by the hypothesis of their authenticity. Jimson admires and emulates Blake, the Blake of the pictures and the prophetic writings. He is not a prophet, though: what counts is his painter's fury and the obstinacy of his refusal to serve.

The Horse's Mouth is the third novel in a trilogy, which was followed by a trilogy in which three overwrought private lives reflect a Lib-Lab progress, a move from radical Liberal to Labour. The three instalments of the earlier trilogy were intended to bring out the mutuality of its three narrators: a big project which did not really come off, as Cary was to feel. *Herself Surprised*, one of his several unfortunate titles, is told by Sara or Sall, a Venus of uncertain allure. She starts as a cook, marries a gentleman, takes up with Jimson and sits for him, and becomes the servant and bedmate of a stuffed shirt by the name of Thomas Wilcher, narrator of the second novel, *To be a Pilgrim*, and the custodian of an ancestral country house, a Wilcher Castle. He thinks of his sister Lucy as his dear friend: characterised as a 'free' rebel, she runs off with an evangelical bigot of tightly closed mind. Tom is at once a liberal and a conservative, for ever shocked by what people tell him. His brother Edward, one of the 'new Liberals' of the first decade of the 20th century, a radical Liberal who soars unsuccessfully to the top of the party pyramid, is deftly done, while Tom seems numbed by his own contradictions.

Sara is a Wife of Bath, who talks of 'God' and 'nature'. Cary mentions her 'soft heart', but such a heart is not always visible. It's possible to feel that Stanley Spencer's golden nude of his malign second wife is Sara to the life, or a portion of her. Having gone to jail for pawning Tom's trinkets, and having made off with a selection of Gulley's works, she is thrown downstairs by the artist, to her death: the second of two deaths in Cary's works that might seem incongruous, more plotted than prepared for, the other being Johnson's execution. For all that, the two get into each other's blood, and Sara says: 'Gulley was the most of a man I ever knew.' When she met him during her period of prosperity he was a shabby 'little bald man with a flat nose and a big chin. His head was big and hung over so that his face was hollow in the middle.' He was to turn out to be 'the instrument of providence, to punish my prosperity and forgetfulness'.

Not only does Jimson throw his former Venus down the stairs, he releases three rats into a crone's shack in order to get at a canvas, and he routinely nicks his patron's netsukes. So why was he so popular in the 1940s and 1950s? There were those at the time – anarchists, bohemians, flower persons before the fact, fans of misrule – who would and must have voted for Jimson, and there were painters who actually resembled him. A discomfort with wartime rules and regulations, along with a nostalgia for the art for art's sake of the previous century, may have entered into the regard for Jimson: Wilde's polemical disjunction of art and morality had not ceased to be influential. But a deference to the sacred monster and other privileged transgressors goes back a long time and is still current, in a number of registers. There is a novel by Anne Tyler about an outbreak of artistic indifference in Baltimore: *Celestial Navigation* (1974) has an artist who has trouble recognising his swarming children, who mislays his wife, and is all for his art. The artist as autist? He is more absent-minded than delinquent, and he is not worshipped. In terms of artistry, and of humanity, Tyler's portrait of the artist strikes me as better than Cary's, but Jimson's narrative is a magnificently explosive Gothic delirium. Jimson and Johnson unite in conveying, like an army with banners, the human cost, not always worth paying, of the practice of art.

Cary's art has other co-ordinates. It gained the interest of two of the foremost novelists of recent times: Saul Bellow in America, and Chinua Achebe, who went to that country from the Nigeria where he grew up. Cary and Bellow – there's a certain brotherliness here. They display a storyteller's interest in human idiosyncrasy which might be thought Dickensian. Neither is allegorical. Both are in different degrees philosophical. Both are comedians. Both are romantic stylists, with Cary the more syntactically loose, prone to parenthesis in later times, and to what Ivy Compton-Burnett called, with regret, 'descriptions', the descriptions other writers went in for. Twenty years after *Mister Johnson*, Bellow published *Henderson the Rain King*. Gene Henderson is a self-centred Yankee millionaire, a married loner who lights out for the African bush in search of his soul and roars with one of its lions – as if in some Reichian orgone box. No such release, no such romantic wisdom, no mysteries, Reichian or Lawrentian, are apparent in Cary's novel, where the *bouquet d'Afrique* chiefly adheres to Johnson's sense of rhythm and his zeal for poetry and parties. From the Africa he encounters – a none too 'correct' joke Africa – Henderson learns lessons in freedom which the adult Larkin would have declined. 'Imagination, imagination, imagination!' cries

Henderson's friend the tutelary African king. Try and be more like a lion! It would be hard to imagine Larkin in a lion's den.

Achebe read *Mister Johnson* as a student in Nigeria, in whose throat 'Rule Britannia' had begun to stick. It gave him the idea that a novel might be written about the way the African countryside truly was and had long been. He also experienced a marked ambivalence towards the novel, as he did towards Conrad's *Heart of Darkness*. The continent was not dark, Conrad caused him to feel; darkness was for foreigners to make much of. 'At the university,' Achebe remarked in 1973, 'I read some appalling novels about Africa (including Joyce Cary's much praised *Mister Johnson*) and decided that the story we had to tell could not be told for us by anyone else no matter how gifted and well-intentioned.' So his first novel was an act of atonement, 'the ritual return and homage of a prodigal son'. In 1972 he had written to somewhat different effect of his start in literature: Cary's novel was 'precisely *the* book that made all the difference. It was the provocation, and the watershed.' Further homage was expressed in *Arrow of God* (1964), where no door to inner deliverance is opened and the chief priest Ezeulu has the skills of a Permanent Under-Secretary in the native land of his Colonial eminence Winterbottom.

These three African books offer very different countries of the mind, different degrees of approximation to the historical reality – each of them, out of Africa, an *aliquid novi*. Achebe's is a homage to his native land which is also a consciousness of the Western novel. In the 1960s he left Nigeria for the universities of the USA. Tribal life had broken up, and Independence had brought to power party bosses who may well have seemed, to some people, enough to stir nostalgia for the Winterbottoms of the past.

Achebe's books are a critique of *Mister Johnson*. But Cary's novel is among his claims to fame. His fiction won him a respected place in his generation of writers, a generation of talented British novelists which has returned to favour in recent years. But then *The Horse's Mouth* has never been away. It's worth revisiting the Larkin of 1945 for a last word on what it was that interested those of its first readers who might have been classed as interested parties. In January of that year he wrote to a friend in Jimsonian vein to say that he once 'stole a Nonesuch Blake from Blackwells (looking back on those days it's a miracle I didn't end in the police court)', and to add that 'nothing means anything to me but writing.' In February he wrote to someone else to say that he'd 'read a good book the other day' – *The Horse's Mouth*. 'Not superlative but managing to catch something of the indomitable soul of art. Really rather moving.'

16

BALTIMORE'S HONEYS

I have never been to Baltimore, but there are moments now when I feel I know it almost as well as I know my native city of Edinburgh, Scotland. But still, I'm a stranger to it, and I feel compunction about referring to the city in a journal based in its vicinity. Baltimore, Maryland, is for me an imaginary city, a Xanadu or Gehenna, and it's also a work of art, due to its presence in the novels of Anne Tyler, of which the latest is *Noah's Compass*, and in the recent television series *The Wire*.[71]

The novels and the series are manifoldly different things. Tyler's novels of manners describe a scene scarcely familiar in *The Wire*, but far from unfamiliar to British eyes. Her Baltimore carries, like some inland scent of the sea, memories of a one-time harbour town, now engulfed by factories, sprawls, malls, suburbs, beltways. There's not much in the way of murder or adultery, while there's a great deal of both in the series. *The Wire* has many black people, while the Tylers have few, most of whom are servants; one of them provides an especially compelling vignette. Family life is fairly inconspicuous in the series, while the novels are preoccupied with it.

In the one case there are gangs, guns, drugs, corrupt police-men, politicians and reporters – all of it lifelike, humanised, dramatised with a power virtually unequalled in contemporary Anglo-American cinema. In the other case there are families, the families of a writer one of whose minor characters is called Joan Derby, an allusion to the proverbial veteran married couple. The novels and the films are works of art which tell between them a tale of two cities, nominally one. What these cities have in common is quarrels.

Unhappy families survive in several of Tyler's fictions, if not always in *Anna Karenina*. Bad mothers, baleful matriarchs, cross adolescents abound, and the barbed impatience of their talk can be startling. Maggie, the sprightly mother in *Breathing Lessons* (1988), with its compelling black man, can sound to herself like an 'elderly, matronly, honey-sweet woman endlessly marvelling and exclaiming'. Tyler's mothers call their children 'honey', but are like Maggie in causing nuisances. And some are the witch herself. Maggie is married to 50-year-old Ira (not as in *Dies Irae*, though there's ire enough in the course of the couple's day trip to a funeral), who 'has never accomplished one single act of consequence', if you discount the containment of his wife's interventions. The marriage survives, but their bid to save their son's marriage fails.

Anne Tyler's commitment to this sore subject of marital and parental tension was announced in her first published novel, *If Morning Ever Comes* (1964). Young Ben Joe goes back for a visit to a household of rude sisters, ruled by a mother who has been deserted by one of the absent husbands who were to recur in Tyler. He takes up with a childhood sweetheart and entrains with her for New York, zestlessly expecting to marry her. Meanwhile a sister's zestless marriage is resumed after a running-away. Nearly everyone is unkind and sharp.

Ben Joe, a 'worrier', snubs his loved ones in a reflexive manner. If he were to vanish, he might perhaps 'not exist' for them. A bleak book, it might seem, *If Morning Ever Comes*. The reader is likely to feel, now and then, that if morning comes night can't be far behind. And yet it's very enjoyable – a characteristic Tyler alchemy takes place, involving an animation of the apparently uninteresting person or nest of persons. The sour mother remarks: 'This family's just like any other family.' Well, yes. It's not unlike other families in Tyler – and in most places.

Dinner at the Homesick Restaurant (1982) enfolds in its title her ambivalence towards family life. No name, this, for a restaurant, but a suitable one for a Tyler novel. As elsewhere, it's 'honey' this and 'honey' that: and here, too, is an unhappy family. Saintly Ezra 'loved his mother dearly but there was something overemotional about her that kept him eternally wary.' His scheming elder brother Cory is eternally jealous of him.

The people in *Saint Maybe*, ten years later, once 'a special family', have 'turned uncertain', 'turned into worriers', thinks the grandmother; and the mother in the earlier book, Pearl, once 'special', is now a prize interfering worrier. She asks a question that Tyler's readers must sometimes ask: 'How come we end up quarrelling? Don't we all love each other?' Her long-absconded untrustworthy husband revisits the fold only to light out again and to deliver an over-eloquent swansong: 'My family wasn't so much,' he'd once thought, 'but it's all there really is, in the end.' There are times when Tyler might seem to accept this, but she can't finally be supposed to do so. There is humour, hers, in the husband's swansong.

'I think it's real holy of you to cast off the superficial, Reverend': *Saint Maybe* has a sympathetic Evangelical minister, founder of the Church of the Second Chance. And it has the Bedloes, who think they're wonderful. Ian is one of the novelist's uncertain saints or innocents, and is characterised by those he looks after, in the manner of Bunyan's *Pilgrim's Progress*, as 'King Careful. Mr Look-Both-Ways. Saint Maybe.' He is one of 'the unremarkable' of whom the Canadian novelist Carol Shields has spoken – who can turn remarkable in, among other writers, Anne Tyler. Their grandmother believes that the Bedloes have become less wonderful with the years: they've turned uncertain. And there's a problem of uncertain paternity with which they have to deal.

The novel mentions a parable which tells of a woman who 'woke up with a man and some children she'd never laid eyes on before', and which intimates that family feelings are 'a matter of blind circumstance'. This may perhaps, and in part, mean that if they're there you look after them, whether or not they're 'yours', and it could appear to be connected with ideas of uncertainty and necessity, and of the loved one as stranger. There's a sturdiness about such uncertainty and families may thrive on it, or at least survive. The minister is liked for being unsure of the advice he gives.

Elsewhere, there's the intimation that families may be a force that dwarfs the matches that perpetuate them: 'this choosing of mates was such a small, brief stage in a family's history.' There's the sense of a necessary survival of the institution, which can overcome mismatch and departure. But it isn't going to overcome the reader's consciousness of the broken marriages there are in the world, and in Tyler.

In her novel of 2006 *Digging to America* two South Korean orphans are respectively adopted by Brad and Bitsy and by Iranian Sami and Ziba. The book consists (to a fault) of a series of anniversary celebrations of the orphans' Mayflower arrival in America. Lots of recipes, and of the domesticity she excels at. 'Entirely alone', Sami's widowed mother is the best of the book. She's a responder with an 'Oh, thank you, but—' to America's invitations and entreaties. The 'no' with which she at first responds to widower Dave's proposal may or may not become a 'yes', to produce, for dynastic necessity, a mixed marriage.

The paradox of family life is related in Tyler's work to this ability of hers to make unpromising people interesting, an ability clearly seen in her latest novel *Noah's Compass*, where a middle-aged schoolteacher, Liam Pennywell, hasn't seemed to have the hang of things and can speak like a stuffed shirt: still, his inhibitions and silences, his unfailing 'Buts', are exasperating but not dull. He's in touch with ungracious daughters and an ex-wife who asks, in an argument with him, 'What is your point, Liam?' By the end of it all, deficiency has been transmuted: this writer's alchemy has been achieved. You see his point.

Not that you are with him all the way. He takes up with a younger woman, but leaves her in the lurch, settling back in his armchair, with 'a book to read. A chicken in the oven.' Relations with his ex-wife appear to be improving. Family life may have been reconstituted.

The Accidental Tourist (1985) is another story of the deserted man who takes up with a younger woman he deserts – but this time he returns to her. The novel is premised on a pirouette, with this swirl of partners. The lightness of the novels can tip over here, as occasionally elsewhere, into a comic levity which can be found to fight with their more disturbing implications. Here, Macon Leary, author of guidebooks to places he doesn't care about, is a maddening, sympathetic compound figure.

Tyler's involvement with the unremarkable or overlooked reveals, in *Back When We Were Grownups* (2001), an interesting dressy widowed Cinderella, an arranger of festivities, whose martyrdom can seem a touch weird. A rich and brilliant book, nevertheless. The same can be said of *A Patchwork Planet* (1998), with its element of contrivance, its overdone detective work, and its appealing black-sheep handyman, divorced Barnaby, who comes to think that it makes no difference whether you've married the right person: 'Finally, you're just with who you're with.'

An earlier novel, *Celestial Navigation* (1974), deals with its family matters by linking them with the portrait of an artist. A Baltimore boarding-house is inhabited by a bohemian mother, a mother nature married for the second time to a personally uninteresting artist who lives for his art and ignores the mounting brood of children at his feet, paying them no more attention than Gulley Jimson does to the people around him in Joyce Cary's definition of genius, *The Horse's Mouth*. This artist could be declared in some respects vacant, but his claims to respect are not quenched by the triumph of the brood that may be impending. The mother casts him off, understand-ably, relinquishing her second chance, but there's the hint of a return. It may be that the Tyler family calculus will hold good: disadvantage, fault, human weakness may defer to the species.

The children in these fictions are bossed and they are often bossy and unruly, and capable of vanishing. A family is its members, but it is also its renegades, its refugees. In *The Amateur Marriage* (2004) Michael, in his Malamud grocer's shop, marries Pauline, and their daughter Lindy runs off with the gypsies – with the hippies of San Francisco. After an absence of legendary duration, she returns to her home, together with adopted children whom she cherishes, though 'no relation to me'. A family doesn't have to consist of blood relations. And blood relations can fall out, just as husbands and wives can become strangers to one another. Lindy's father comes to feel that with Pauline he is 'standing next to a stranger'. One day, just like that, he deserts her, and reflects: 'Imagine! Once this woman and I were married.' It was as if 'I'd been another person back then. I'd been this distant acquaintance I'd heard of who married a woman named Pauline a long, long time ago.' And yet the last page of the novel has him dream that he is hurrying towards her house, after his second wife's death.

Tyler's account of marriage can include a perspective that might recall the accents of Jacobean drama, those of John Ford's *The Lover's Melancholy*:

> For he is like to something I remember
> A great while since, a long, long time ago.

I remember the lines from a great while since, and it's possible that Tyler was remembering them when she wrote as she does here.[72] She does not write tragedies, but her comedies are not free from pain: and yet her account of marriage can often seem accepting, affirmative. The most striking of her runaways is the heroine of *Ladder of Years* (1995), who heads off from her inattentive husband and her children, forms no further attachments, and resumes with the inattentive husband. Here, as in Tyler's account of family life, an apt complexity is explored. What she does is put before us what goes wrong in the families we have to have, the woe there can be in the marriages that need to be made, and may bring happiness.

Lindy's flight, along with others of a similar sort, is iconic for the recent North American novel. Alice Munro, Carol Shields and Philip Roth have all written about the principled female vagrant. Shields's Ontario girl is found sitting on a pavement with matted hair and a sign saying 'Goodness'. A controlling holy man may be interviewed in such works, a reverend with a knife beneath the cloak, and they can give an impression at times of the writer's anxiety – of a fear that art had estranged a blood relation. The homestead is defended against the dissident, who can also be a terrorist. Home is best, but then home may also be guilty.

It's not surprising that it should require an anarchic extremism to call for the abolition of families. In the Sixties the British anthropologist Edmund Leach offended his compatriots by speaking in the BBC's Reith Lectures of the 'tawdry secrets' of the family. Since then, families have rarely been publicly defamed in Britain – certainly not by politicians. 'Hard-working families', as opposed to bankers and hustlers, are almost all the Labour government of 2009 had to hold on to, with the Tory opposition no less familial, after its own fashion. Margaret Thatcher was understood to believe that the family is all-important and that there is no such thing as society. Do Tyler's books say the same? The family goes on, in her books; and the range of Baltimore life, together with the Maryland polity, goes unstressed. But the blights and faults visible in the narrower focus of family life are more than conceded.

They are part of a comedy of errors charged with verbal felicity – a dimension of her writing to which I haven't done justice, in my eagerness for theme. Witness the words of *Morgan's Passing* (1980), with its artist-like compulsive impostor; and of *The Clock Winder* of 1972. This has its witch, a crisis merchant who complains that her children '*live* on crisis', and it has her tomboy handyman Elizabeth, who does not care, and a son of the house, Timothy, who tells acquaintances that he has drowned his gerbil and has kept ants: but 'you have no idea how silly it makes you look with the neighbours. "I'll be out of town a few days, could you water my ants?"' Finely evoked, Timothy of the little jokes and round, puckered, defeated face does not thrive. The tussling Stimsons of the novel are a wonderful near-approach to Dickens's Smallweeds.

Tyler is a quiet and a modest writer, with much to be immodest about. It may be that she has no one masterpiece among her books. Her collected works, in their entirety, their sustained excellence, are her masterpiece.

NOTES

1   *The Country and the City*, pp. 231, 217, 248, 256. *Border Country*, 1988 ed., pp. 133, 145.

2   See Kilvert's *Diary 1870–1879*, paperback 1964. This volume, edited by William Plomer, was derived from his three-volume selection from the diaries, published in 1938, 1939 and 1940.

3   *Kilvert, the Victorian: A New Selection from Kilvert's Diaries*, ed. David Lockwood, 1992, p. 286.

4   *Francis Kilvert and His World* by Frederick Grice, 1983, p. 237.

5   Plomer, 1964 ed., pp. 241–2.

6   See Grice, p. 71; Lockwood, pp. 53, 55.

7   Plomer, 1964 ed., pp. 253, 293.

8   Grice, pp. 174, 218, 226; Lockwood, p. 14. And see V.S. Pritchett's *Collected Essays*, 1991, p. 79.

9   Grice, p. 218.

10 Plomer, 1964 ed., pp. 268, 277–8.

11 Ibid., p. 280

12 Ibid., pp. 30–1.

13 *Lark Rise to Candleford*, 1954 ed., p. 556. *The Wheelwright's Shop*, 1923, p. 25.

14 *Akenfield*, paperback ed. 1972, pp. 76, 313, 294, 232.

15 *Mr Weston's Good Wine*, 1928 ed., pp. 57, 182. *Cold Comfort Farm*, paperback 1938, p. 69.

16 Plomer, 1964 ed., p. 244.

17 'Postscript', *Opened Ground: Poems 1966–1996*, p. 444.

18 See *Mrs Woolf and the Servants* by Alison Light, 2007, p. 246.

19 *Cambridge Today*, Michaelmas Term 1951.

20 See *Henry Vaughan: A Life and Interpretation* by F.E. Hutchinson, 1947, pp. 170, 228.

21 See his poem 'On Lord Holland's Seat near Margate, Kent'.

22 *South of the River*, pp. 303, 364.

23 *Nature's Cure*, p. 128.

24 *Natural Mechanical*, pp. 38–40. *The Testament of Cresseid* and *Seven Fables* by Robert Henryson, translated by Seamus Heaney, 2009.

25 *At the Bright Hem of God*, 2009, pp. 217, 193, 211.

26 *On the Crofters' Trail*, pp. 111–15, 146.

27 *Creatures of the Earth: New and Selected Stories*, 2006.

28 *The View from Castle Rock* appeared in 2006.

29 See *Electric Shepherd* by the present writer, revised ed. 2005, pp. 225, 167.

30 Published in Toronto in 2002.

31 *On Chesil Beach*, 2007.

32 See *Authors* by the present writer, 1989, p. 51.

33 *Stepping Stones: Interviews with Seamus Heaney* by Dennis O'Driscoll, 2008.

34 *Seamus Heaney: In Conversation with Karl Miller*, Between the Lines, 2000.

35 *Birthday Letters*, 1998. The letters are addressed to the deceased Sylvia Plath.

36 *A Life of James Boswell*, 1999.

37 *Lord Cockburn: Selected Letters*, Edinburgh, 2005.

38 *Lord Cockburn: A Bicentenary Celebration 1779–1979*, Edinburgh, 1979.

39 *Patrick Sellar and the Highland Clearances* by Eric Richards, 1999, gives a robust account of Sellar's activities, from a point of view

broadly sympathetic to his conception of the economic case for the Clearances. See also the 'Report of the Trial of Patrick Sellar', 1816, British Library, Rare Books. This report offers a defence view of what happened in court.

40 See *Ian Niall: Part of his Life*, by his son Andrew McNeillie, 2007, p. 85.

41 *Lark Rise to Candleford*, 1954 ed., p. 56.

42 *A Galloway Childhood*, pp. 57, 4.

43 *Wigtown Ploughman*, pp. 23, 25.

44 *The Poacher's Handbook*, pp. 20, 97.

45 *Wigtown Ploughman*, pp. 26–7, 345.

46 *Alasdair Gray: A Secretary's Story*, 2008.

47 See the 2007 edition.

48 See pp. 217, 194–5.

49 The poem, written with Peter Kelly, is given in *The Dear Green Place* and *Fur Sadie*, edited and introduced by Alasdair Gray, 2008. The second of these is published in the Gray edition for the first time.

50 Published respectively in 1993 and in 1998.

51 'Marion's Jock' is included in a Penguin Classics edition of the *Confessions* (2006) done by the present writer.

52 There have been more.

53 See Jeremy Cater's editorial introduction, p. xiii, to *The Invention of Scotland: Myth and History*, 2008.

54 *Letters from Oxford to Bernard Berenson*, by Hugh Trevor-Roper, ed. Richard Davenport-Hines, 2006, p. 82. *Historical Essays* by Hugh Trevor-Roper, reissued 1966, pp. 208–9, 202. *The Invention of Scotland*, p. 76.

55 *Letters to Berenson*, p. xvii.

56 *The Invention of Scotland*, p. 204.

57 Ibid., pp. 18, 150.

58 *Scotland's Books*, 2007, p. 129.

59 *The Invention of Scotland*, p. 181.

60 See *Electric Shepherd* by the present writer, 2003, p. 256.

61 *The Invention of Scotland*, pp. 178–9.

62 *Letters to Berenson*, p. xx.

63 The *Invention of Scotland*, p. 202.

64 Ibid., pp. 216–17, 221.

65 *Historical Essays*, p. 64.

66 *Letters to Berenson*, p. xxxviii.

67 Ibid., p. xix.

68 See Andrew O'Hagan's *The Atlantic Ocean*, 2008.

69 *What to Look for in Winter*, 2010.

70 *Herself Surprised, Charley is My Darling, Except the Lord, The Horse's Mouth, Castle Corner, Not Honour More, Prisoner of Grace, To be a Pilgrim, Mister Johnson*, 2009.

71 *Noah's Compass* was published in Britain in 2009. The journal referred to is *Raritan*, based in New Brunswick, New Jersey.

72 *The Lover's Melancholy*, 4:3. The lines were once well-known, under the influence, perhaps, of T.S. Eliot's exploration of the Jacobean playwrights.

INDEX

229